The Dark Night

Psychological Experience
AND
Spiritual Reality

ICS Publications
2131 Lincoln Road NE
Washington, DC 20002-1199
www.icspublications.org

© Washington Province of Discalced Carmelites, Inc., 2018

Published with Ecclesiastical Approval

All Scripture passages are taken from the *New Revised Standard Version: Catholic Edition, Anglicized Text*, © 1999, 1995, 1989, Division of Christian Education of the National Council of Churches of Christ in the United States of America. Used with permission.

Back cover author photo © Randy Hill, 2016, published with permission; R.B. Hill Photography, LLC: www.rbhillphoto.com.

Cover and book design and pagination by Rose Design

Produced and printed in the United States of America

Library of Congress Cataloging-in-Publication Data

Names: Foley, Marc, 1949- author.
Title: The dark night : psychological experience and spiritual reality / Marc Foley, O.C.D.
Description: first [edition]. | Washington DC : ICS Publications, 2018. | Includes bibliographical references and index.
Identifiers: LCCN 2018050005 | ISBN 9781939272799 (alk. paper)
Subjects: LCSH: John of the Cross, Saint, 1542-1591. Noche oscura del alma. |
  Mysticism--Catholic Church. | Psychology, Religious.
Classification: LCC BV5082.3.J65 F65 2018 | DDC 248.2/2--dc23
LC record available at https://lccn.loc.gov/2018050005

ISBN 13: 978-1-939272-79-9

10 9 8 7 6 5 4 3 2 1

THE
Dark
Night

PSYCHOLOGICAL EXPERIENCE AND SPIRITUAL REALITY

MARC FOLEY, O.C.D.

ICS Publications
Institute of Carmelite Studies
Washington, D.C.

OTHER BOOKS BY MARC FOLEY, O.C.D.

The Ascent of Mount Carmel: Reflections
ICS Publications, 2013

St. Teresa of Avila – The Book of Her Foundations: A Study Guide
ICS Publications, 2011

*The Context of Holiness: Psychological and Spiritual Reflections
on the Life of St. Thérèse of Lisieux*
ICS Publications, 2008

The Path to Merciful Love: 99 Sayings by Thérèse of Lisieux
New City Press, 2007

Peace of Heart: Reflections on Choices in Daily Life
New City Press, 2007

A Season of Rebirth: Daily Meditations for Lent
New City Press, 2007

The Story of a Soul by St. Thérèse of Lisieux: A Study Edition
ICS Publications, 2005

The Ascent to Joy: St. John of the Cross
New City Press, 2002

*The Love That Keeps Us Sane:
Living the Way of St. Thérèse of Lisieux*
Paulist Press, 2000

*In gratitude to my dear friend Sandra Gettings
for her invaluable advice and suggestions*

CONTENTS

Book Two

FOREWORD

～∽◡∽～

Try to read *The Dark Night* by St. John of the Cross and you will experience a variety of reactions. It does that to anyone searching for wisdom on the path to God, and consequently it is a deeply engaging undertaking. The poem itself, written shortly after his escape from a horrendous captivity in 1578–1579, is filled with striking imagery that challenges the reader to follow him on the path to wholeness. Darkness and light, grace and love, fill the journey John poetically describes. Traces of his stunning escape reverberate throughout the first five stanzas, while the remaining three stanzas bring to mind one of the other poems he wrote while in his dank prison cell. The prose treatise he completed most likely while in Granada in 1584 follows in the path of *The Ascent of Mount Carmel*, which he completed around the same time. Strikingly, John abruptly ends both treatises without explanation. Why did he stop? Did he feel he had explained the process enough? Was it because he felt drawn to a more mystical prose that he used in his two later main commentaries on the poems *The Spiritual Canticle* and *The Living Flame of Love*? We may never know, but nonetheless his treatise on *The Dark Night* reveals to us St. John of the Cross's incredible insight into the human psyche and God's working in and with the human being, drawing the person ever more deeply into the divine life God yearns to share with all. Despite what one might feel while reading his writings, St. John of the Cross was always practical and rooted in life experience: his own life and the lives of those with whom he came into contact.

Reading *The Dark Night* can be a daunting task. The intricacies of the actual process that St. John of the Cross describes as God brings the human being closer and closer to full participation in the gift of God's own life might be confusing. However, it is perhaps the sheer darkness and demands involved in the purgations of which he speaks in this work that can make one think it is an impossible path for all but the most elite. Moreover, the language of sixteenth-century Spain is not the language of the twenty-first-century person living in a completely different context. Combined with this, our lives built around the chatter of technology, comfort, and ease do not prepare us well for seeing into the depths of who we really are and who we are intended to be as fully alive human beings. St. John of the Cross accents the need of deeper silence if we are to move beyond our comfort zones and dare to look with deep humility at the person we have made ourselves and see the need to let go and make space for God. The description of the dark night of faith that John presents seems so stark and painful that one hesitates to read it. Face-to-face with this, it is no wonder that we become fearful and stop reading him, consoling ourselves with the notion that such a lofty path is not meant for us. However, it is this painful darkness that opens a whole new, wonder-filled world of light for all.

We are indeed fortunate to have this book by Discalced Carmelite Father Marc Foley to guide us through the pathways to full life that St. John of the Cross portrays in *The Dark Night*. Father Marc opens St. John of the Cross's deep understanding of the experiences and graced events in the process of letting go to be truly alive in God, as God's children. By his statements, quotations from a myriad of writers both ancient and modern, and by his questions, Father Marc lays bare the human being's hidden agendas, which was St. John's purpose as well in writing this work. Moreover, he unveils the depth and meaning of St. John of the Cross's language by emphasizing certain words used in Spanish and explaining what they meant in John's time and what they mean today. And he does this without ever being tedious, boring, or pedantic.

Father Marc clearly shows the key elements in St. John of the Cross's approach to explaining the process of life with God as the *inflow* of God. In this journey what may seem to be regression is more likely progress: not one's own progress but God's work of loving and becoming more and more alive in the person. What appears to be and is experienced as utter darkness is in fact the light revealing the closeness of God—known only in faith. This is truly what we find in all the great Carmelite holy ones of all time: a life of faith lived no matter how we define darkness. Being weaned of total dependency on our senses, we find newness and light in the seeming darkness. This inflow in the inner depths of the person is contemplation: gift of the Godself to all who believe in love.

Father Marc, like St. John of the Cross, understands the human psyche and so he makes John more accessible to people today. His own theological background, his experience as a spiritual guide, his own journey in life, and his knowledge of St. John of the Cross equip him to write this wonderful guide. Like John, Father Marc knows the human being and the challenge of becoming fully human and fully alive. As he writes we find ourselves challenged to look at what it really means to be human—and what we are meant to be as we live out our lives. Through both Father Marc and St. John of the Cross we read and reflect on how God moves, acts, and lives with us day by day. We see the persistence of God, of God's love pursuing us until finally we surrender and dare to be as God: reflections of the divine in every facet of our lives.

Father Marc Foley's approach provides every reader with the proper attitude to read St. John of the Cross profitably. He opens the texts of St. John with his perspicacious look at the most troublesome phrases and words that are unfamiliar terrain to the contemporary reader. In doing so he unveils the hidden treasures that lie within them. At the end of each section, he provides what he calls "For Reflection." Here he highlights the main points of the previous part and asks the reader questions that help to see more personally the meaning of what St. John of the Cross hoped to communicate. Without a doubt, this book by Father Marc Foley is one of the best ones available to engage any reader, regardless of one's background in the process of the life-giving journey to God, with God, and in God.

PROFESSOR RICHARD P. HARDY
SAN DIEGO, CALIFORNIA

PREFACE

Experience is always an interpreted experience. [Thus] the interpretation makes the experience to be what it is for us. . . . Suppose, for example, that I am walking at night along a dimly lit street and suddenly a group of six young men cross over from the other side of the street and come in my direction. . . . At that moment the experience for me [is] one of apprehension. . . . I cannot but wonder whether these are the same men who, according to newspaper reports, have been terrorizing this neighborhood in recent weeks. . . . But, as the group comes closer, I recognize them as students of mine who are coming over to say hello. . . . Suddenly my interpretation of the situation changes drastically; I no longer see them as a menace. I feel assured rather than threatened. . . . The changed interpretation has made my personal experience entirely different.[1]

These words of theologian Bernard Cooke point to a fundamental fact about daily experience. We do not have an experience and *then* interpret it. Rather, how we interpret an event shapes how we experience it. In short, all experience is interpreted experience, and there is a reciprocal cause-and-effect relationship between thoughts and emotions; our thinking shapes our feelings, and our feelings impact our interpretations of reality.

We tend to interpret reality through our emotions. In this regard, we are apt to think that if something *feels* good, it must *be* good, and if something *feels* bad, it must *be* bad. Although the "feel good/be good, feel bad/be bad" interpretation of experience is sometimes valid, many times it is erroneous. This is never truer than in the spiritual life. For example, in *The Dark Night of the Soul*, St. John of the Cross points out that when we *feel* that God is *absent*, it is often the case that God is more *present* in our soul.

Throughout *The Dark Night*, John helps us to interpret spiritual experiences according to reality, namely, how grace operates within us. Since we are prone to interpret spiritual reality through our emotions, knowledge of John's interpretations of the effects of grace is crucial for all of us seeking guidance on the spiritual path.

This book is based upon my reading of John's works and my experience of working with numerous individuals in spiritual direction. It is my prayer that you who read this book will gain insight into John's wisdom that will help you to find guidance on your spiritual journey home to God.

ORIENTATION FOR THE READER

I n October 1571, as St. Teresa of Ávila was in the midst of establishing convents for her reform, she was ordered back to the convent of the Incarnation in Ávila to serve as prioress. The community that numbered approximately 180 nuns had grown lax, and the monastery was on the brink of financial ruin. In "the midst of this whole Babylon" (Ltr 1.38.4), as Teresa called the Incarnation, it was necessary for her to impose discipline upon the community. This measure was met with fierce resistance, as one might expect. As Teresa put it, "Changing a habit is like death" (Ltr 1.38.4). Teresa needed help, so the following year, she arranged to have St. John of the Cross serve as the confessor and chaplain for the nuns. During the next five years, which he considered some of the happiest years of his life, John ministered to the nuns and the local church. Unfortunately, during these tranquil years in Ávila, a storm was brewing within the Carmelite Order. Teresa's reform was beginning to be held suspect. So much confusion, misunderstanding, and animosity surrounded the canonical and jurisdictional rights of Teresa's foundations that many Carmelite friars wanted to put an end to Teresa's experiment.

It was within this context that John was abducted by his Carmelite brothers and taken to Toledo where he was told to renounce Teresa's reform. Because he refused, John was imprisoned in a six-by-ten-foot cell for nine months. The living conditions were wretched. The cell was unsanitary and unventilated, and he was given barely enough food to survive. It was within these horrendous conditions that John composed some of his greatest poems, most notably *The Spiritual Canticle* (the first thirty-one verses), "Stanzas of the Soul that Rejoices in Knowing God through Faith," and the *Romances*.

One moonless night, after nine months of imprisonment, John made a harrowing escape from his prison cell. After loosening the screws on his prison door, he waited until 2:00 a.m., when everyone was asleep, and then he tiptoed to an adjacent room that had a balcony. He tied a rope that he had made from two blankets to the railing of the balcony and lowered himself down. The rope was too short, which meant that he had to swing a little in order to land on the wall below. The wall was only two feet wide. If he had missed the wall or had lost his balance, he would have fallen to certain death on the jagged cliffs of the Tagus River.

In the darkness, he made his way to the convent of the Carmelite nuns in Toledo. They took him in, fed him, and bathed his wounds. Then, they secretly arranged to have John placed in a nearby hospital where he recuperated for six weeks. From his hospital room, John could see the balcony window of the monastery from which he had made his escape. It is thought that during this time John wrote the poem *The Dark Night*.

Years later, John shared this and other poems with the Carmelite nuns of Beas. The nuns were so moved by his poems that they asked John to explain them. He did so orally, by means of homilies and conferences. Gradually, he put down his thoughts in writing, which became his commentaries on his poems. His commentaries on the poem *The Dark Night* are *The Ascent of Mount Carmel* and *The Dark Night of the Soul*.

John did not foresee writing commentaries on his poetry. Moreover, since the commentaries and poetry were written independently of one another, the connection between the two is tangential at best. As theologian George Tavard writes in *Poetry and Contemplation in St. John of the Cross,* John's commentaries "wander a considerable distance from the text [of the poem], which is then partially relegated to the role of 'pretext.'"[1] In consequence, the poem and the prose commentary can be, and perhaps *should* be, read separately.

APPROACHING THE POEM

As you read the poem *The Dark Night,* clear your mind of all preconceived ideas regarding its meaning. Allow the images of the poem to resonate in your spirit and listen to what they evoke within you. Allow God to fashion in you a "deep and delicate listening" (F 3.34).

1. One dark night,
fired with love's urgent longings
—ah, the sheer grace!—
I went out unseen,
my house being now all stilled.

2. In darkness, and secure,
by the secret ladder, disguised,
—ah, the sheer grace!—
in darkness and concealment,
my house being now all stilled.

3. On that glad night,
in secret, for no one saw me,
nor did I look at anything,
with no other light or guide
than the one that burned in my heart.

4. This guided me
more surely than the light of noon
to where he was awaiting me
—him I knew so well—
there in a place where no one appeared.

5. O guiding night!
O night more lovely than the dawn!
O night that has united
the Lover with his beloved,
transforming the beloved in her Lover.

6. Upon my flowering breast
which I kept wholly for him alone,
there he lay sleeping,
and I caressing him
there in a breeze from the fanning cedars.

7. When the breeze blew from the turret,
as I parted his hair,
it wounded my neck
with its gentle hand,
suspending all my senses.

8. I abandoned and forgot myself,
laying my face on my Beloved;
all things ceased; I went out from myself,
leaving my cares forgotten among the lilies.

In Louisa May Alcott's novel *A Modern Mephistopheles*, Gladys Carnaris says to her poet husband Felix, "I think you will never do better; for this [poem] came from your heart, without a thought of what the world would say. Hereafter all you write may be more perfect in form but less true in spirit, because you will have the fear of the world, and loss of fame before your eyes."[2]

There is much truth here. English psychiatrist Anthony Storr contends that composers, artists, and poets who reach a level of maturity enter into what he calls the "Third Period," in which they produce their greatest works. The works of this period "are characterized by an absence of rhetoric or any need to convince. . . . [They] seem to be exploring remote areas of experience which are intrapersonal or suprapersonal. . . . [They are] looking into the depths of [their] own psyche[s] and [are] not very much concerned as to whether anyone else will follow or understand [them]."[3]

The spiritual truth contained in these words is that when our ego is purified of the need to impress others and our spirit is transformed by grace, our words flow from the depths of our souls. John composed *The Dark Night* in such a state. He is explicit in this regard. "Before embarking on an explanation of these stanzas, we should remember that the soul recites them when it has already reached the state of perfection—that is, union with God through love—and has now passed through severe trials and conflicts by means of the spiritual exercise that leads one along the constricted way to eternal life . . . called a dark night" (N Prol 1).

Having passed through the dark night, John's ego is purified; he has no need either to impress or convince anyone of his truth. He is not a poet who needs a following because he has "lost the herd that [he] was following" (C 26). However, John offers us a suggestion regarding reading his poems. They should be "read with the simplicity of the spirit of knowledge and love they contain" (C Prol). In short, they should be read in the same spirit in which they were written.

This may be a difficult task for those of us who have made our first acquaintance with John's poetry in conjunction with his commentaries. We may be reading John's poems through the lens of his prose. Such an approach constricts our imagination by binding John's poetic imagery with the strictures of conceptual knowledge.

John bids us to read his poems with the heart rather than the mind, since they were "composed with a certain burning love of God . . . [which] overflow in figures, comparisons and similitudes" (C Prol 1). Furthermore, he explicitly invites us to interpret his poems from our own experience.

"It is better to explain the utterances of love in their broadest sense so that each one may derive profit from them according to the mode and capacity of one's own spirit, rather than narrow them down to a meaning unacceptable to every palate. As a result, though we give some explanation of these stanzas, there is no reason to be bound to [my] explanation" (C Prol 2).

APPROACHING THE COMMENTARY: THE SITUATION OF THE READER

In stave 1 of *A Christmas Carol*, two portly gentlemen, in an effort to raise money for the poor, come to Scrooge's counting house in the hope of obtaining a donation. Scrooge flatly refuses, arguing that the poor are lazy. Scrooge considers himself a realist and a shrewd man of business. After he turns the two gentlemen out, Scrooge "resumed his labours with an improved opinion of himself and in a more facetious temper than was usual with him."[4] However, as Scrooge does so, Charles Dickens reveals to the reader what has happened within Scrooge's soul.

> Meanwhile the fog and darkness thickened so, that people ran about with flaring links, proffering their services to go before horses in carriages and conduct them on their way. . . . The cold became intense. In the main street, at the corner of the court, some labourers were repairing the gas-pipes, and had lighted a great fire in a brazier, round which a party of ragged men and boys were gathered: warming their hands and winking their eyes before the blaze in rapture. The water-plug being left in solitude, its overflowings sullenly congealed, and turned to misanthropic ice.[5]

Scrooge's self-congratulatory frame of mind blinds him to the coldness that has congealed in his soul, or as John would say, "Gladness is blinding to the heart and does not allow it to consider and ponder things" (A 3.18.5). Although Scrooge is unaware of the state of his soul, the reader understands the truth—Scrooge's heart has turned to ice.

The reader has this understanding because Dickens wrote from a third-person omniscient point of view. In works of literature, a third-person omniscient narrator stands above the story with an all-knowing perspective and an all-encompassing understanding. As readers, we stand above the text with the narrator and see through his eyes.

The Dark Night of the Soul has the characteristic of a third-person omniscient point of view. As readers, we stand above the text with John as he interprets the deep workings of grace within our souls. Just as Dickens reveals the contrast between Scrooge's spiritual condition and his *misinterpretation* of it, so too John reveals our spiritual reality in contrast to our emotional interpretations.

For example, often beginners *believe* they are holy because they *feel* holy, due to consolation. However, their feelings blind them to their spiritual reality. Their belief in their holiness makes them unaware of their pride and self-righteousness. "They develop a somewhat vain—at times very vain—desire to speak of spiritual things in others' presence, and sometimes even to instruct rather than be instructed . . . in their hearts they condemn others who do not seem to have the kind of devotion they would like them to have. . . . [They are not] aware that all [their] works and virtues are not only worthless . . . but even become vices" (N 1.2.1–2).

Because these beginners equate their feelings with reality, they are not conscious of their true spiritual condition. Like beginners, we all tend to interpret the spiritual by means of the emotional. Throughout *The Dark Night of the Soul*, John, our third-person omniscient narrator, discloses to us the spiritual reality that lies beneath our erroneous emotional interpretations. Like the protagonist in Leonard Cohen's song "Hallelujah," John tells us "what's really going on below."

Translation and Abbreviations

St. John of the Cross

All quotations of St. John of the Cross are taken from *The Collected Works of St. John of the Cross*, translated by Kieran Kavanaugh, O.C.D., and Otilio Rodriguez, O.C.D. (Washington, D.C.: ICS Publications, 1991). The abbreviations for John's works are as follows:

A   *The Ascent of Mount Carmel*
C   *The Spiritual Canticle*
Co   *The Counsels*
F   *The Living Flame of Love*
N   *The Dark Night of the Soul*
Pre   *The Precautions*
SLL   *The Sayings of Light and Love*

Regarding references to both *The Ascent* and *The Dark Night*, the first number indicates the book; the second number refers to the chapter, and the third number refers to the paragraph. For example, A 2.3.4 refers to book two, chapter 3, paragraph 4 of *The Ascent*. Similarly, for *The Spiritual Canticle* and *The Living Flame of Love*, the first number refers to the stanza and the second number to the paragraph. Thus, C 3.4 is a reference to stanza 3, paragraph 4 of *The Spiritual Canticle*.

St. Teresa of Ávila

All quotations of St. Teresa of Ávila are taken from the Kieran Kavanaugh, O.C.D., and Otilio Rodriguez, O.C.D., translation of *The Collected Works of St. Teresa of Avila*, 3 vols. (Washington, D.C.: ICS Publications, 1976–1985). The abbreviations for St. Teresa's works are as follows:

F   *The Book of Her Foundations*
IC *The Interior Castle*
L   *The Book of Her Life*
Ltr *The Collected Letters*, volumes 1 and 2
W   *The Way of Perfection*

For *The Book of Her Life, The Interior Castle, The Way of Perfection,* and *The Book of Her Foundations,* the first number refers to the chapter, and the second number refers to the paragraph. Thus, L 3.5 refers to *The Book of Her Life,* chapter 3, paragraph 5. Regarding *The Interior Castle,* the first number refers to the dwelling place; the second number refers to the chapter; and the third number refers to the paragraph. Thus, IC 3.4.2 refers to the third dwelling place, chapter 4, paragraph 2.

St. Thérèse of Lisieux

All quotations of St. Thérèse of Lisieux are taken from the John Clarke, O.C.D., translation of her works by ICS Publications. The abbreviations for St. Thérèse's works are as follows:

S   *Story of a Soul*
L   *The Collected Letters*
LC *The Last Conversations*

The number following the letter refers to the page of the ICS Publications edition of the work cited. Thus, S 13 refers to page 13 of *Story of a Soul* (third edition.)

BOOK ONE

NIGHT 1.1

Introduction to
the Imperfections of Beginners

~ ⌒ ~

When beginners have been "resolutely converted" (N 1.1.2), God strengthens their resolve by showering them with consolation. God acts "like a loving mother who warms her child with the heat of her bosom, nurses it with good milk and tender food, and carries and caresses it in her arms" (N 1.1.2). In consequence, beginners find joy in the things of God. "The soul finds its joy, therefore, in spending lengthy periods at prayer, perhaps even entire nights; its penances are pleasures; its fasts happiness; and the sacraments and spiritual conversations are its consolations" (N 1.1.3).

Although these spiritual activities are good, they are "the habits of childhood" (N 1.1.2) because, like children, beginners are motivated by pleasure. "Their motivation in their spiritual works and exercises is the consolation and satisfaction they experience in them" (N 1.1.3). The "arduous struggle of practicing virtue" (N 1.1.3) only begins when God withdraws the emotional support that consolation provides. When God "withholds her caresses and hides her tender love . . . and sets the child down from her arms, letting it walk on its own feet" (N 1.1.2), the dark night commences. Here, John helps us to distinguish

3

the *emotional* from the *spiritual*. All of our explicitly religious activities are not necessarily spiritual, for we can perform them "because of the satisfaction attached to [them]" (N 1.1.3).

Also, John unmasks one of the great misconceptions of the spiritual life, namely, if something is *religious* it must be *spiritual*. One of the great dangers in the conversion process is substituting one attachment for another. In John's drawing of Mount Carmel, there are three paths going up the mountain. The path in the center leads to the top of the mountain; it is the path of detachment. The path on the right side, which leads us astray, is called "the goods of earth." It consists of *joy, knowledge, consolation, and rest.* The path on the left side, which leads us astray, is called "the goods of heaven." It consists of *joy, knowledge, consolation, and rest.* Sometimes what seems like a spiritual conversion amounts to little more than a lateral shift from the "goods of earth" to the "goods of heaven."

TEXTS AS MIRRORS

St. Augustine's *Confessions* had a profound impact on the conversion of St. Teresa because she saw her life mirrored in the text. "As I began to read the *Confessions*, it seemed to me I saw myself in them. . . . When I came to the passage where he speaks about his conversion and read how he heard that voice in the garden, it only seemed to me, according to what I felt in my heart, that it was I the Lord called." (L 9.103)

Many of us can attest to a similar experience. Some books have acted like mirrors for our lives. Not only have they reflected back to us our own experience, but also they have served as catalysts to change. Perhaps this is what John intended in his portrayal of the faults of beginners (chapters 2 through

7), for he tells us that he will "first mention here some characteristics of beginners . . . [so that they] will . . . *desire* that God place them in this night" (N 1.1.1; italics added).

John's psychologically and spiritually astute analysis can pierce us with a shaft of self-recognition, which in turn can evoke within us a desire to enter a process of conversion.

Although his treatment of beginners can prove to be embarrassingly revelatory, his purpose is not to shame us but to heal us. Healthy shame "is potentially medicinal," writes sociologist Helen Merrell Lynd, for it "may throw an unexpected light on who one is and points the way toward who one might become."[1] This is John's intent—to shed light on our darkness.

How embarrassed we feel when we realize that we have "develop[ed] . . . a very vain desire to speak of spiritual things in others' presence" (N 1.2.1). At such moments, we become aware of what we had been blind to before. "My God, they were embarrassed *for* me, and I couldn't see it." Or how conscience-stricken we feel when we realize we have "become so evil-minded that [we] do not want anyone except [ourselves] to appear holy; and so by both word and deed condemn and detract others" (N 1.2.1). Or how mortified we feel when we realize how transparent is our play-acting. "Sometimes they want others to recognize their spirit and devotion . . . [and thus] contrive to make some manifestations of it, such as movements, sighs, and other raptures, more in public than in private . . . eager for others to take notice of these" (N 1.2.3).

As you read the chapters on the imperfections of beginners, pay attention to your emotional reactions. In what way does the text function as a mirror? In what way do your reactions motivate you to *want* God's purifying grace to enter your soul?

CONSOLATION AND THE CAPITAL SINS

The presence of God as consolation is meant to be an *aid* to spiritual advancement. Unfortunately, it often becomes an *obstacle*. "Some others let themselves be encumbered by the very consolations and favors God bestows on them for the sake of their advancing, and they advance not at all" (A Prol 7). What hinders spiritual advancement is not consolation per se but our relationship to it. We can become attached to the sensual experience of consolation; we can develop "a spiritual sweet tooth" (A 2.7.5) and become addicted to the spiritual savor of grace. As a result, our capacity to embrace the cross is diminished.

We can also misinterpret the significance of consolation. Many beginners believe that what they *feel* is an indication of their holiness; they think they are saints because they find great delight in their spiritual exercises. John deals with these two hindrances within the framework of the seven capital sins.

As creatures made in the image and likeness of God, our deepest inclination is to seek God. However, because we are infected by original sin, we also have an inclination to seek our ultimate good in objects that are less than God. The specific inclinations of the will that seek objects that are less than God are called the capital sins (pride, envy, anger, sloth, avarice, gluttony, and lust).

For one person, pride may be the strongest inclination, whereas for another, it may be lust. In addition, the strength of a particular inclination may be strong in one person and less so in another. Thus, John writes that these imperfections are "serious in some people . . . yet others have little more than the first movements toward them. But there are scarcely any beginners who at the time of their initial fervor do not fall victim to some of these imperfections" (N 1.2.6).

These inclinations are often triggered by situations in our lives. For example, an inclination toward envy, which has lain dormant for years, can be triggered by the success of a colleague or friend. In John's chapters on the imperfections of beginners, the seven capital sins are triggered by an experience of God in the form of consolation. But how can an experience of God's presence cause an inclination toward sin? It doesn't. Consolation is not the cause of the imperfections of beginners; it is the catalyst. It can stimulate an addiction to pleasure and can trigger pride.

For the next six chapters, John considers the imperfections of beginners, and although he deals with them within the framework of the seven capital sins, they can all be subsumed under the dangers of pride and addiction to sensual pleasure.

Finally, it is important to keep in mind that even though John is dealing specifically with "beginners," the psychological and spiritual insights into the dynamics of the capital sins that are contained in these chapters can apply to all of us.

For Reflection

In this chapter, John tells us that beginners desire to experience God as consolation. There is nothing wrong with this desire, for who of us does not want to experience God's consoling presence?

Unfortunately, one of the dangers with this desire is that it can become so inordinate that our primary "motivation in [performing] spiritual works and

CONTINUED

exercises is the consolation and satisfaction [that we] experience in them" (N 1.1.3). If this happens, our behavior can become so dependent upon feelings that we will "lose the spirit of perseverance" (A 3.28.7). Conversely, writes St. Teresa, if we are "paying little attention" to whether we have "much consolation or no consolation," we "have traveled a great part of the way" (L 11.13).

In one sense, we are all "beginners," for every day we are faced with the decision to be faithful to prayer regardless of whether it is consoling or dry.

What have you found to be helpful to strengthen your resolution regarding your faithfulness in prayer?

NIGHT 1.2

Spiritual Pride

~~~⌁~~~

The term "beginner" is a misnomer, for John's beginners have already begun to walk the spiritual path. They "practice meditation" (N 1.1.1) and are engaged in spiritual "exercises" (N 1.1.3). As an aid to their budding efforts, God showers them with consolation. "It should be known, then, that God nurtures and caresses the soul *after* it has been resolutely converted to his service" (N 1.1.2; italics added).

Although God is not restricted to when he imparts consolation, John's statement that consolation is given after beginners have begun the spiritual journey may be significant. Perhaps John is alluding to one of the reasons beginners frequently interpret the experience of consolation from an egocentric perspective. Since it is given after they have exerted a considerable amount of energy in establishing their spiritual practices, it would be reasonable to conclude that consolation is a reward that God is bestowing upon their efforts. St. Teresa says something similar when she writes, "[Since] consolations arise from the virtuous work itself that we perform . . . it *seems* that we have earned them through our own effort" (IC 4.1.4; italics added). As a result, beginners see themselves as God's favorites, which in turn engenders spiritual pride. John begins his treatment of spiritual pride

9

with the following statement. "These beginners feel so fervent and diligent in their spiritual exercises and undertakings that a certain kind of secret pride is generated in them that begets a complacency with themselves and their accomplishments" (N 1.2.1).

How can religious fervor and diligence in the performance of spiritual exercises produce complacency? One would think that the opposite would be true. The answer to this seeming contradiction lies in the beginner's erroneous image of holiness. They mistake perfection of outward observance with perfection of charity. They cannot see that even though fidelity to one's religious exercises is important, it pales in comparison with the weightier demands of holiness: charity, mercy, kindness, forbearance, forgiveness, and humility. Since beginners are fervent in outward observance, they are satisfied or complacent with their progress in the spiritual life.

Their smug complacency, which is rooted in their observant concept of holiness, is the basis out of which they "condemn others who do not seem to have the kind of devotion they would like them to have" (N 1.2.1). They feel justified in the harshness of their judgments because they are based upon hard facts—the observance of the law. It is not by accident that John says the "criticism [of beginners is] like the pharisee who despises the publican while he boasted and praised God for the good deeds he himself accomplished" (N 1.2.1).

Although none of us may be actual pharisees, we do have something in common with beginners: our judgments of others are sometimes rooted in our ideas of what constitutes holiness.

THE BLINDNESS OF BEGINNERS

As beginners feel fervor in performing their spiritual exercises, they do not recognize their pride because it is often experienced as humble gratitude. "God, I thank you for what you have done for *me*." The hidden implication of this "humble" prayer is that they are singularly blessed. At first, their pride is not expressed openly, which is itself an expression of pride. They pride themselves on the belief that they do not have a need that others know of their unique relationship to God. Because their "secret pride . . . begets a complacency with *themselves*" (N 1.2.1; italics added), they do not feel a need to make an outward show of their "holiness"—at least temporarily.

However, as their inflated self-image grows, their pride begins to shape their outer demeanor. They don the persona of a saintly sage. "They . . . speak of spiritual things in others' presence and sometimes even instruct [others]" (N 1.2.1). By doing so, they attempt to enhance their reputation as wise and holy people and become threatened by anyone who appears to be either more knowledgeable or holier than themselves.

Feeling threatened, they begin to so interject themselves into conversations that they won't even let a person finish a sentence. "When [they] notice that someone is trying to give them some instruction, they themselves take the words from their very mouths as though they already know everything" (N 1.2.7). They are oblivious to the fact that this habit grates on the nerves of others. They do not notice when people either stand before them in cold silence or heave a sigh of exasperation. Some beginners are so proud and oblivious to their faults that it takes a public humiliation to wake them up. Sometimes this happens when another person loses patience and erupts in exasperation: "For heaven's sake, will you be quiet and let me finish what I'm saying! Do you think that you're the only person who knows anything? Do you have any idea of how much you turn people off?" Such remarks can be a moment of grace. As St. John Climacus writes, "Because of our unwillingness to humble ourselves, God has arranged that no one can see his own faults as clearly as his neighbor."[1]

DISSIMULATION

Another manifestation of the threatened pride of beginners is vicious envy, which finds voice in detraction. "Some of these persons become so evil-minded that they do not want anyone except themselves to appear holy; and so by both word and deed they condemn and detract others whenever the occasion arises" (N 1.2.2). As they tear others apart, they simultaneously seek to regain center stage. They do so by engaging in ostentatious displays of piety that border on the theatrical. "[They] want others to recognize their spirit and devotion, and as a result occasionally contrive to make some manifestations of it, such as movements, sighs, and other ceremonies . . . they experience raptures, more often in public than in private, and they are quite pleased, and often eager, for others to take notice of these" (N 1.2.3).

These beginners are unaware that it is blatantly obvious to others that their behavior is contrived. In fact, people do take notice of them but not in the way that they either expected or desired. All their posturing, play acting, and simulation render them embarrassingly ridiculous in the eyes of others.

According to John, they also attempt to impress others by their carefully crafted speech. They paint themselves in the best possible light and so censor anything that would challenge the image of holiness they try to project. They even conceal their sins in the very act of confessing them.

> Many want to be the favorites of their confessors, and thus they are consumed by a thousand envies and disquietudes. Embarrassment forbids them from relating their sins clearly, lest their reputation diminish in their confessor's eyes. They confess their sins in the most favorable light in order to appear better than they actually are, and thus they approach the confessional to excuse themselves rather than accuse themselves. Sometimes they confess the evil things they do to a different confessor so that their own confessor might think they commit no sins at all. Therefore, in their desire to appear holy, they enjoy relating their good behavior to their confessor, and in such careful terms that these good deeds appear greater than they actually are. (N 1.2.4)

"Fond of the respect of the wise and good among my fellowmen . . . I committed [myself] to a profound duplicity of life."[2] These words of Dr. Henry Jekyll, taken from Robert Louis Stevenson's novella *The Strange Case of Dr. Jekyll and Mr. Hyde*, capture the tragedy in the above passage. When we have an inordinate desire for human respect, to be the "favorites" of others, or are afraid that our "reputation diminish" (N 1.2.4) in their eyes, there is a great danger that we can embark upon a life of duplicity. And the danger never becomes more real than when we achieve the reputation we desire. For then, don't we feel burdened with keeping up appearances and living in fear of being unmasked? There is much truth in Oscar Wilde's words, "When the gods wish to punish us they answer our prayers."[3] If beginners are not placed in the dark night, the habit of cloaking the truth can grow, for "not to go forward on this road is to turn back, and not to gain ground is to lose" (A 1.11.5).

Fragile Image

The whole emotional life of these beginners is consumed by the need to have their image of holiness recognized. They need to be regarded as special; they fear embarrassment, and they envy others. Their self-esteem revolves around their inflated self-image. However, their puffed-up image is easily punctured. This is because they experience a discrepancy between their "ideal self" and their "real self"; their imperfect behavior clashes with their exalted self-image.

This conflict is manifested in their vacillating reactions to their faults. Sometimes they "minimize their faults," and at other times, "they become discouraged by them" (N 1.2.5). One moment they believe they are "already saints" (N 1.2.5), and the next moment they "become impatient and angry with themselves" because they are not saints (N 1.2.5). Both the minimization of their faults and the anger at their faults are manifestations of pride.

Minimization is a form of rationalization that protects one's self-image by either denying or playing down one's faults and failings. Likewise, anger at one's faults "is yet another fault" of pride (N 1.2.5). It is a reaction of self-hate in the service of one's exalted self-image. As psychiatrist Karen Horney writes, "The very condemnation of imperfection confirms the godlike standards with which the person identifies himself."[4] Or as St. Francis de Sales writes regarding the source of inordinate anger towards our imperfections, "It springs from no other source than self-love."[5]

Anger toward one's imperfect self is an insidious form of pride that can cloak itself in the guise of humility. It proclaims to the world, "Look how humble I am!" There is much truth in what Mr. Darcy says in Jane Austen's novel *Pride and*

Prejudice: "Nothing is more deceitful than the appearance of humility . . . [it is] an indirect boast."[6] Feigning humility is a ploy of pride.

People who belittle themselves in public often do so to elicit praise. This happens when their normal means of obtaining a compliment fails. They get so frantic for any crumb of recognition that they present themselves as pitiful. They beg others to supply them with the admiration that they so desperately need. John compares them to the foolish virgins in the Gospel. "Sometimes they even seek [praise]. In this they resemble the foolish virgins who had to seek oil *from others* when their own lamps were extinguished [Mt 25:8]" (N 1.2.5; italics added).

BEGINNERS AND HUMILITY

Not all beginners are afflicted with spiritual pride. John tells us that some beginners who experience consolation "are advancing in perfection" (N 1.2.6) because they are humble *before* they experience consolation. "Since they are truly humble, their growing fervor and the increased number of their good deeds and the gratification they receive from them only cause them to become more aware of their debt to God" (N 1.2.6).

By pointing out the fact that when some beginners experience consolation they interpret it from an egotistical perspective whereas others do not, John is indicating an important fact about the relationship between consolation and pride. Consolation doesn't cause spiritual pride; it is a catalyst. It triggers pride that already exists in the beginner. Conversely, beginners who are humble before they experience consolation grow in gratitude for the gift they have been given.

THE DARK NIGHT

A FINAL CONSIDERATION

As we come to the end of our consideration of John's analysis of spiritual pride in beginners, it is important to realize that when God withdraws consolation from them and they enter into the dark night, the capital sin of pride is not eradicated. At best, beginners acquire self-knowledge regarding the glaring manifestations of spiritual pride that they exhibited when they experienced consolation. However, spiritual pride is not the exclusive domain of beginners.

Let us consider Joe, a "beginner," who, when showered with consolations, exhibited all the manifestations of spiritual pride that John writes of in this chapter. When God withdrew consolation, Joe was initially confused. However, after reading *The Dark Night of the Soul*, he realized that his supposed "holiness" was simply an emotional "high" and that authentic sanctity required an "arduous struggle of practicing virtue" (N 1.1.3).

Joe was duly humbled and took to heart John's teaching. Through perseverance, he grew in the virtues, and he began to experience the peace of a disciplined life. This was an important milestone in Joe's spiritual journey. Unfortunately, he began to pride himself on his ascetical achievements and felt a secret joy when he saw that so many of his peers lacked the self-discipline that he had acquired.

Just as consolation triggered spiritual pride in Joe when he was a beginner, so too did the peace that virtue affords trigger spiritual pride in him when he became a proficient. Spiritual pride is mercurial by nature; it assumes different forms and becomes harder to detect the more that it counterfeits virtue. We find an example of how the virtue of simplicity, coupled with spiritual idealism, is transmuted into a refined form of pride that cloaks itself in humility in the character of Dorothea Brooke, the protagonist of George Eliot's novel *Middlemarch*.

Dorothea's simplicity of life and her high ideals make her attractive. However, these characteristics become prey to her pride, which manifests itself in a judgment of anything that she deems to be either mundane or worldly. We see this in a conversation that Dorothea has with her sister Celia.

When their mother died, Celia and Dorothea inherited her jewels. One day, Celia suggested that they divide their mother's jewels between themselves. When they opened the jewelry box, they discovered a beautiful cross that was studded with fine pearls. When Celia proposed that Dorothea should have it, Dorothea gasped.

> "Not for the world, not for the world. A cross is the last thing I would wear as a trinket." Dorothea shuddered slightly.
>
> "Then you will think it wicked in me to wear it," said Celia uneasily.
>
> "No, dear, no," said Dorothea, stroking her sister's cheek. "Souls have complexions too: what will suit one will not suit another."
>
> Celia felt a little hurt. There was a strong assumption of superiority in this puritanic toleration, hardly less trying to the blond flesh of an unenthusiastic sister than a puritanic persecution.[7]

As an example of spiritual pride, John references the pharisee in the Gospel who boasted of his righteousness as he looked down his supercilious nose at the publican (N 1.2.1). Don't we see an echo of this parable in Dorothea's exchange with Celia? Isn't Dorothea's assumption of superiority and her tolerance of Celia's worldliness a manifestation of patronizing pride? Perhaps Dorothea's refusal to wear a "worldly trinket" is how she dons her pride, for we are told that she was in the custom of wearing plain dresses that set her apart from others. "Her plain garments, by the side of provincial fashion, gave her the impressiveness of a fine quotation from the Bible."[8]

Dorothea's choice not to be decked out in the world's finery was itself a statement. It proclaimed to the world her unworldliness. Dorothea might have gained some self-knowledge into her behavior if she had known of St. Jerome's admonition: "In dress avoid somber colors as much as bright ones. Showiness and slovenliness are alike to be shunned; for the one savors of vanity and the other of pride."[9] Or as St. Augustine writes, "Vainglory can find a place, not only in the splendor and pomp of worldly wealth, but even in the sordid garment of sackcloth as well, and that it is then all the more dangerous because it is a deception under the pretense of service of God. . . . [Its purpose is in] attracting men's attention to his manner of professing Christianity."[10]

Some people wear pride like a necklace (Ps 73:6). Others take pride in not wearing one. Although pride can manifest itself in many ways, those who are prideful have one thing in common. They all search for glory; they all strive to be praised and esteemed by others.

For Reflection

Regarding pride, Blaise Pascal writes that when "we are not satisfied with the life that we have . . . we wish to live an ideal life in the minds of others, and for that

CONTINUED

purpose put on appearances. We labor incessantly to adorn and sustain this ideal being, while neglecting the real one."[11]

Likewise, some beginners are obsessed with what other people think of them; they labor incessantly to acquire a reputation for holiness in the minds of others. They "desire to speak of spiritual things in others' presence" (N 1.2.1) and have a "readiness to perform" acts of piety in order to "appear holy" (N 1.2.2). They want to be "regard[ed] . . . with esteem and praise" and have people "congratulate them and be impressed by their deeds"(N 1.2.3). They have a need to "appear better than they actually are" (N 1.2.4).

Have you ever attempted to acquire a reputation for holiness?

Have you ever experienced the heavy burden that keeping up the appearance of holiness entails?[12]

In his essay "On the Cannibals," Michel de Montaigne begins by noting the "horrible barbarity" of certain tribes of cannibals in Brazil. However, he says that, in one sense, his own culture is more barbaric than the Brazilian cannibals. "I think there is more barbarity in eating a man alive than in eating him dead . . . and what is worse [we do it] in the name of duty and religion."[13] Under the name of religion and holiness, certain beginners "become so evil-minded that they do

CONTINUED

not want anyone except themselves to appear holy; so by both word and deed they condemn and detract others whenever the occasion arises" (N 1.2.1).

Detraction is eating a person alive; it is "biting at another's reputation in secret," as St. Thomas Aquinas says (*Summa Theologiae* [ST] II–II, q. 73, a. 1). It is a sin that can be camouflaged easily under the guise of holiness and honesty because the detractor is telling the truth. Detraction is different from calumny. Calumny tells lies about others, whereas detraction reveals the truth about another. Detraction is an unwarranted disclosure of a hidden fault or failure of another, which tarnishes that person's reputation.

Have you ever been "so evil-minded" that out of either envy or spite you deliberately tarnished another person's reputation?

NIGHT 1.3

Spiritual Avarice

⁓⚬⁓

Many beginners also at times possess great spiritual avarice. They hardly ever seem content with the spirit God gives them. They become unhappy [*desconsolados*] and peevish [*quejosos*] because they don't find the consolation they want in spiritual things. Many never have enough [*no se acaban*] of hearing counsels, or learning spiritual maxims, or possessing and reading many books about them. They spend more time in these than in striving after mortification and the perfection of the interior poverty to which they are obliged. Furthermore, they weigh themselves down with overdecorated images and rosaries. They will now put these down, now take up others; at one moment they are exchanging and the next re-exchanging; now they want this kind, now they want another. (N 1.3.1)

J ust as the root problem of spiritual pride is an inflated ego, so too the root problem of spiritual avarice is an insatiable id. The former is an addiction to an exalted self-image; the latter is an addiction to sensual pleasure. Beginners inclined to spiritual pride interpret the experience of consolation from a narcissistic perspective, whereas beginners who are predisposed to spiritual avarice have an insatiable thirst for the sensual gratification that consolation provides.

In both cases, they are driven by what they seek to avoid. Just as the spiritually proud perform all of their deeds to be seen because they are petrified that they will not be the center of attention, so too the spiritually avaricious crave for consolation so they don't become bored.

In this chapter, John deals with two types of beginners who are addicted to consolation. The first we will call the *spiritual dilettante*; and the second, the *spiritual collector*.

THE SPIRITUAL DILETTANTE

Many beginners who are afflicted with spiritual avarice can "never have enough [*no se acaban*] of hearing counsels, or learning spiritual maxims, or possessing and reading many books about them" (N 1.3.1).

They believe that their insatiable hunger is spiritual because the sources from which they derive consolation are explicitly religious. They fail to recognize that what they label as "spiritual" is merely emotional. These beginners do not crave insights for the sake of spiritual growth; rather, they are addicted to the stimulation that novelty provides. They are excited by something that is new; this is why they are forever picking up one book and laying it down for another.

They are driven by what they are trying to avoid: boredom. When they are not experiencing consolation, "they become unhappy [*desconsolados*] and peevish [*quejosos*]" (N 1.3.1). *Desconsolados* can be translated as disconsolate, downcast, inconsolable, sad, or depressed, whereas *quejosos* can be translated as querulous, cross, testy, irritable, peevish, or touchy. In short, they are restless. Their avaricious pursuit of consolation in the form of intellectual stimulation is a way of coping with their inner agitation. They are gluttons for emotional experiences that they hope will assuage their sense of boredom and emptiness.

In our own day, spiritual dilettantes can take the form of people who flit, to and fro, from one workshop to another that promises self-knowledge. One week, they are enthusiastic about what they have learned in a seminar on the Myers-Briggs, and the following week, they are scurrying off to a workshop on the Enneagram. They are collectors of ideas and systems of thought that they can talk about with their friends but never apply to their own lives. They love to ingest information but do not have the capacity to do the hard and tedious work that is required to digest it. They love to hear counsels, learn spiritual maxims, and read books about them. Their craving for intellectual stimulation is insatiable. The Spanish, "*no se acaban*," that is translated in the above passage "never have enough," may also be rendered, "There's no end to it."

Spiritual dilettantes love to talk about the books they have read, the places they have traveled, and the rich variety of spiritual systems of thought to which they have been exposed. If this tendency is not mortified by grace in the dark night, there is a danger that they can become dabblers who skate on the surface of life, who taste everything because they do not possess the perseverance to digest anything. They lack the capacity to go deeply into any subject in case they become bored. The enthusiasm of spiritual dilettantes is unbridled curiosity that St. Thomas Aquinas calls a "roaming unrest of spirit."[1]

This form of spiritual avarice may best be understood as the vice of curiosity or vain inquisitiveness. Curiosity, according to Scholastic philosophy, is an unbridled, unregulated, undirected appetite for knowledge that results in a distracted mind and an inattentive spirit. It is an addiction to intellectual excitation; it is not about acquiring knowledge in the pursuit of truth. "Curiosity is about the *pleasures* arising from knowledge acquired" (Thomas Aquinas, *Summa Theologiae* [ST] II, II, q. 167, a. 2; italics added).

However, when the pleasurable excitement of newly acquired ideas quickly wanes, these beginners feel empty. In turn, their emptiness goads them on to another indiscriminate search for stimulation. This is why spiritual dilettantes are never content and are forever ravenous.

However, there is a deeper emptiness that ensues from their inordinate, indiscriminate appetite for stimulation than the temporary one they feel between pursuits. It is a void of meaning because their accumulated knowledge is devoid of purpose, beyond intellectual stimulation, and an ostentatious display.

In contrast, there are beginners who "do not care to know any more than is necessary to accomplish good works, because their eyes are fixed only on God, on being his friend and pleasing him. . . . Their pleasure is to know how to live for love of God. . . . They set their eyes on the substance of interior perfection, on pleasing God and not themselves" (N 1.3.2).

Their pursuit of knowledge, like that of the spiritual avaricious, provides them with pleasure. However, their pleasure brings purpose into their lives because it is in the service of their ultimate end—"how to live for love of God" (N 1.3.2). Furthermore, they are free from the careworn drive of acquiring more and more knowledge. "They do not care to know any more than is necessary" (N 1.3.2). They are content with what they know, unlike the spiritually avaricious who "hardly ever seem content" (N 1.3.1).

THE SPIRITUAL COLLECTOR

> Furthermore, they weigh themselves down with overly deco-
> rated images and rosaries; they will now put these down, now
> take up others; at one moment they are exchanging and the
> next re-exchanging; now they want this kind, now they want
> another (N 1.3.1).

Beginners who collect religious objects are no different than
those who love to hear counsels and learn spiritual maxims.
Although the objects of their choices differ, one of the reasons for their avarice seems to be the same, the avoidance of
boredom. Both are restless and agitated. Just as spiritual dilettantes seek excitement in new ideas, so too spiritual collectors
seek excitement in the novelty of a religious object that is striking, original, or unusual. Just as spiritual dilettantes take up
one book to put it down for a more stimulating one, so too
spiritual collectors "put [one religious object] down to take up
others; at one moment they are exchanging and the next re-
exchanging" (N 1.3.1).

Spiritual collectors often consider themselves aesthetes
who pride themselves on their refinement and taste. However, they are blind to the fact that their emphasis on "over-
decoration" and "elaborateness" (N 1.3.1) often renders them
ridiculously garish as they parade around "weigh[ed] down
with overdecorated [*curiosos y vistosos*] images and rosaries" (N
1.3.1). *Curiosos* can be translated as odd, novel, or exotic, and
vistosos means showy.

John paints a picture of a friar standing before his bedroom
mirror trying to decide which rosary or religious object he will
wear that day. "[He] will now put these [images and rosaries]
down, now take up others; at one moment [he is] exchanging

and the next re-exchanging; now [he] want[s] this kind, now [he] want[s] another" (N 1.3.1).

John's concern is not with the embarrassing, ostentatious display of these beginners but with the spiritual consequences of their attachments. Since their minds are riveted on a life of show, "their eyes are [not] fixed on God" (N 1.3.2). Being "decked out . . . like children in trinkets . . . [they cannot grasp] . . . the substance of devotion" (N 1.3.1).

There are two reasons these beginners are oblivious to their condition. First, because the objects they are attached to are explicitly religious, they are unable to perceive their possessiveness. Second, they cannot differentiate authentic spiritual devotion from aesthetic satisfaction. John writes of these two types of blindness in *The Ascent of Mount Carmel*.

> "Perhaps these images are more dangerous, for in saying 'they are holy objects' these persons become more assured and do not fear natural possessiveness and attachment. Spiritual persons are thus at times seriously deluded by thinking they are filled with devotion because of their satisfaction in the use of these holy objects." (A 3.38.1)

As with spiritual pride, spiritual avarice doesn't automatically disappear the moment the novice leaves the novitiate or the beginner ceases to be a beginner. Although he may have shed his trappings that made his cell look like a curio shop and his habit an eye-turner on the runway of religious fashion, this does not mean the capital sin, that is, the *inclination* toward avarice, has been mortified. It may have evolved into a more refined and sophisticated form. His desire to strut around in an overly deco-rated habit may have metamorphosed into an inordinate appetite to display his exquisite "taste" in all things religious. He may no longer collect religious objects but rather ideas on religious art.

Now he struts around, draped in his overly decorated ego, displaying his discriminating taste and eye for aesthetic refinement.

Since there is a kinship between beauty and holiness, these people assume their refined sense of aesthetics mirrors their holiness. However, their real situation is disclosed by their testiness when either their "taste" is called into question or their pride is threatened by the presence of a rival. At such moments, they are unmasked. Their refinement is disclosed as the veneer of their egos, rather than a substantial quality of soul.

CONCLUSION

Beginners infected with spiritual avarice, whether spiritual dilettantes or spiritual collectors, are in danger of becoming spiritually sterile. They are blind to this danger because they cannot distinguish intellectual and aesthetic sensibilities from authentic spirituality.[2] Again, John helps us to differentiate the spiritual from the emotional; he helps us to see beneath the facade of the spiritually avaricious, whose focus is on the outer shell of religiosity rather than on the "substance of . . . devotion" (N 1.3.1).

When John writes that spiritual collectors "weigh themselves down [se cargan] with overdecorated images and rosaries" (N 1.3.1), he is referring to not the physical weight of religious objects but the psychic and spiritual burden that they carry. *Cargan*, derived from *cargar*, means to load, to burden, or to carry, as a ship carries cargo.

Both spiritual dilettantes and spiritual collectors are weighed down with an inordinate concern for their image in public. They are weighed down with the burden of keeping up appearances. It is their cargo, their baggage that they lug through life.

In contrast, beginners who are "intent on the substance of the devotion" (N 3.1.2) are not loaded down with these concerns. In fact, the opposite is true. They have become "tire[d] of all . . . multiplicity and elaborate ornamentation" (N 1.3.1). They have become weary of the burden of an ornamental life.

For Reflection

"Where is the wisdom we have lost in knowledge? Where is the knowledge we have lost in information?"[3] These words of T. S. Eliot speak of the spiritual damage that many beginners inflict upon themselves. Since they "never have enough of hearing counsels, or learning spiritual maxims, or . . . reading many books about them" (N 1.3.1), they become spiritually malnourished. Their minds become noisy and cluttered with information that is a barrier to receiving God's quiet wisdom. Their ravenous appetite for information prevents them from digesting the truths that are set before them. There is much truth in Edmund Burke's words, "Reading without reflecting is like eating without digesting."

One of the core issues contained in this chapter is our purpose for acquiring knowledge. Do we want to know in order to increase our stockpile of information, or do we want to receive the wisdom "to know how to live for love of God and neighbor" (N 1.3.2)? Why do you read spiritual material, to acquire information or

CONTINUED

to seek God's guidance? How do you read, with haste or slowly and meditatively? It would benefit all of us to heed John's counsel: "Seek in reading and you will find in meditation" (SLL 158).

NIGHT 1.4

Spiritual Lust

First, [lustful thoughts and feelings] often proceed from the pleasure [*gusto*: pleasure, delight, gratification] human nature finds in spiritual exercises. Since both the spiritual and the sensory part of the soul receive gratification [*gusta*] from that refreshment [*recreación*: recreation, relief, diversion, amusement], each part experiences delight [*deleitarse* from *deleitar* to delight, to please or have pleasure in] according to its own nature and properties. The spirit, the superior part of the soul, experiences renewal [*recreación*] and satisfaction [*gusto*] in God; and the sense, the lower part, feels sensory gratification [*gusto*] and delight [*deleite*] because it is ignorant of how to get anything else, and hence takes whatever is nearest, which is the impure sensory satisfaction. (N 1.4.2)

It is not uncommon to become sexually aroused during prayer. "Without a person being able to avoid it, impure movements will be experienced in the sensory part of the soul, and even sometimes when the spirit is deep in prayer or receiving the sacraments of Penance or the Eucharist" (N 1.4.1). John says that these movements have three causes.

The first is the psychosomatic unity of our nature, or to use the language of Scholasticism, we are a "whole harmonious composite" (N 2.11.4) or "one suppositum" (N 2.1.1). In short, we are so constructed that our mental life has an impact upon both our emotions and our bodies. For example, when we are mentally agitated, we become emotionally distraught, which changes our biochemistry, which in turn affects our physical health. We all know this from experience. The stress of daily life, which weighs down upon the mind, gives rise to physical ailments such as high blood pressure and lower back pain. Conversely, research has shown that a peaceful mind promotes physical health. When we are mentally relaxed, the activity of the sympathetic nervous system is reduced, which in turn lowers the stress hormones (adrenaline, cortisol, etc.).

Similarly, when we experience consolation in prayer, both the body and spirit will "receive gratification [and] refreshment [*recreación*] . . . according to its own nature. . . . [The spirit] experiences renewal [*recreación*] and satisfaction in God; [however, the body] experiences sensual rebellions, movements, and acts in the senses" (N 1.4.2).

John does not tell us explicitly why the gratification and refreshment that the spirit receives from consolation trigger sexual arousal in the body. However, he does give a clue. He emphasizes that the spirit experiences *recreación* or relief. This relief, when communicated to the body, results in muscular relaxation. When our muscles relax, the sexual tension that is trapped in our bodies is released. This can give rise to "sensual rebellions and movements."

The second cause of these movements and rebellions of the flesh is the devil, who parades before our mind's eye images that can tempt us to sin. However, the primary purpose of the devil's temptations is not to lead us into sin but to induce us to abandon prayer. "Through fear, some souls grow slack in their prayer—which is what the devil wants—in order to struggle against these movements, and others give it up entirely, for they think these feelings come while they are engaged in prayer rather than at other times. And this is true because the devil excites these feelings while souls are at prayer, instead of when they are engaged in other works, so that they might abandon prayer" (N 1.4.3).

This passage shows the devil's cunning. He uses our desire to struggle against temptation for the purpose of abandoning the very means of overcoming temptation. We find an example of this diabolical strategy in the life of St. Teresa of Ávila. When Teresa was living a "worldly" life in the Convent of the Incarnation, going "from pastime to pastime, from vanity to vanity," she was tempted by the devil, under the guise of humility, to give up the practice of mental prayer. "This was the most terrible trick the devil could play on me, under the guise of humility: that seeing myself so corrupted I began to fear the practice of prayer. It seemed to me that, since in being wicked I was among the worst, it was better to go the way of the many, to recite what I was obliged to vocally and not to practice mental prayer" (L 7.1–2). After Teresa understood the nature of the devil's wiles, she realized that he was tempting her to give up the very means to remedy her "worldly" life.

> I recount this also that one may understand how if the soul perseveres in prayer, in the midst of the sins, temptations, and the failures of a thousand kinds that the devil places in its path, in the end . . . the Lord will draw it forth to the harbor of salvation. . . . I can speak of what I have experience of. It is that in spite of any wrong they who practice prayer do, they must not abandon prayer since it is the means by which they can remedy the situation; and

to remedy it without prayer would be much more difficult. May the devil not tempt them, the way he did me, to give up prayer out of humility. (L 8.4–5)

This passage from Teresa's *Book of Her Life* helps us to understand the gravest danger that spiritual lust poses to us. It is not indulging in sexual fantasies but giving up the spiritual means of overcoming them. When we are plagued with "foul and impure thoughts" (N 1.4.3) during prayer, we can become so frightened by their sheer strength that we are unable to recognize the temptation to abandon prayer. This leads us into the third cause of these movements and rebellions of the flesh: fear. "The third origin from which these impure feelings usually proceed and wage war on the soul is the latter's fear of them. The fear that springs up at the sudden remembrance [*súbita memoria*] of these thoughts, caused by what one sees, is dealing with, or thinking of, produces impure feelings" (N 1.4.4).

To understand why our fear is the cause of what we fear, we have to understand the nature of the fear. "The fear . . . springs up at the sudden remembrance [*súbita memoria*] of these thoughts." *Súbita* can mean sudden, unforeseen, or unexpected. Thus, it is not merely the remembrance of these thoughts that causes the fear but also our inability to guard ourselves from their unpredictable appearance. We become afraid because we feel vulnerable and unprotected in the face of our own memory from which there is no escape. At any moment, without warning, impure thoughts and feelings that are recorded in the memory can be triggered into consciousness.

The only recourse we feel we have is to try to repress these memories. In the process, the situation becomes worse because avoidance is a form of attention. The more we try not to think of something, the more we think of it. For example, if I said, "Close your eyes, and for the next fifteen seconds try not to think of pink elephants," what would you be thinking of?

Pushing thoughts out of our mind is like pushing down a spring. It will recoil because it has been coiled. We give power to the things we repress. As St. Francis de Sales counsels, "Do not force yourself to conquer your temptations, for those efforts will strengthen them."[1] This raises a question. Considering that we should neither dwell upon nor repress impure images that arise in our minds, how should we relate to them?

The unknown author, a fourteenth-century mystic, of *The Cloud of Unknowing* offers us a way out of this dilemma. In regard to distractions in prayer, he writes, "When distracting thoughts annoy you, try to pretend that you do not even notice their presence or that they have come between you and your God. Look beyond them—over their shoulder, as it were."[2]

Looking over the shoulder of distractions or looking beyond them avoids the two extremes of repressing and focusing upon them. It is accepting the fact that a distraction is staring you in the face but choosing not to look into its eyes. We cannot blot a distraction out of our minds anymore than we can avoid seeing a person who is standing directly in our line of vision. However, we can avert our gaze.

This method of dealing with distractions is like seeing an alluring object out of the corner of one's eye but choosing not to look at it. This spiritual discipline makes us grow in love. As the author of *The Cloud of Unknowing* puts it, this practice "amounts to a yearning for God. . . . And desire like this is actually love."[3]

It is comforting to know there is no guilt attached to the sexual images and feelings that spontaneously present themselves to our conscious mind. As John writes, "These impure feelings [are] outside one's control" (N 1.4.1). "The fear that springs up at the sudden remembrance of these thoughts . . . produces impure feelings without the person being at fault" (N 1.4.4).

John calls thoughts that arise spontaneously in our minds "first movements." Not only can they do us no harm if we "look over their shoulder," but also, by doing so, we grow in virtue. "Insofar as one resists them, one wins strength, purity, comfort, and many blessings, as our Lord told St. Paul: *Virtue is made perfect in weakness* [2 Cor 12:9]" (A 1.12.6).

This is a very important truth to remember as sexual images and feelings arise in our minds because we frequently feel we are being defiled. However, this is not the case. As John writes, although the "passion and disturbance [temptations] momentarily cause make it seem that one is being defiled and blinded, such is not the case; rather, they occasion the opposite good effects" (A 1.12.6). It is comforting to realize that our erotic feelings and the sexual images that arise in our minds are one means by which we can grow in the virtue of chastity and the love of God.[4]

SPIRITUAL CONVERSATIONS

The audience that beginners who are infected with spiritual pride try to impress is generic in nature. They "speak of spiritual things in *others'* presence" (N 1.2.1); they "want *others* to recognize their spirit and devotion [and want] *others* to take notice of [them]" (N 1.2.3; italics added). Beginners in whom spiritual pride is intermingled with spiritual lust often want to impress specific individuals. Their "spiritual conversations . . . manifest a certain sprightliness [*brío*] and gallantry [*gallardía*] on considering who is present" (N 1.4.6).

Brío encompasses qualities such as strength, valor, and manliness, and *gallardía* contains connotations of gallantry and bravery. Within the context of John's culture, these are chivalric or knightly qualities. Therefore, it is a reasonable assumption that the specific manifestation of spiritual lust that John is referring to is of a man trying to impress a woman.

John seems to be referring to very egocentric men. He tells us that when they are engaged in their "spiritual conversations . . . they carry on with a kind of vain satisfaction [*vano gusto*]" (N 1.4.6). *Vano gusto* may best be translated as a smug self-satisfaction.

This self-congratulatory frame of mind blinds these beginners to the real motives and desires that lurk within their "spiritual" conversations. They only become aware of their motives and desires upon reflection. "This lustful origin will be recognized if, on recalling that affection, there is remorse of conscience, not an increase in the remembrance and love of God" (N 1.4.7).

This passage reflects the human condition so well. Often when we are alone, we recognize the underlying motives and desires of our behavior. How often have we thought that our relationships with certain individuals were purely "spiritual," when our fantasy life reveals to us the truth? At such times, we stand naked before our lusts and our egotism. "The shame of motives late revealed,"[5] to use T. S. Eliot's words, is a shattering but salutary experience. As it shatters our illusions about our holiness, it brings in its wake "remorse of conscience" (N 1.4.7). It is a redemptive moment when "the laws of remorse are restored," as songwriter and poet Leonard Cohen speaks of in his song "Amen."

This is an experience of the dark night, for the "inflow of God [comes] into the soul . . . purg[ing] it of its habitual ignorances" (N 2.5.1). John, our third-person omniscient guide, reveals to us the workings of grace operating within the searing and merciful pain of self-knowledge. The inflow of God that enlightens the secret motives of our hearts and burns us with remorse is a great grace. However, it does not transform us; it only enlightens us. Being purged of our habitual ignorances, or what we call "blind spots," only makes us aware of what needs to be healed and transformed. Healing occurs when we cooperate with grace, when we choose to act upon insight. The choices we must make in order that God may heal us are also the work of the dark night, for "God teaches the soul secretly and instructs it in the perfection of love" (N 2.5.1). Whether we heed or turn a deaf ear to God's voice is our choice.

For Reflection

John tells us that one of the ways of recognizing that a relationship in not entirely spiritual is "if, on recalling that affection, there is remorse of conscience" (N 1.4.7). We have an example of this in the life of St. Teresa of Ávila.

When Teresa was a young religious, she developed a relationship with a priest named Pedro Hernández, in which they "conversed a great deal . . . of the things of God" (L 5.4). Upon reflection, Teresa realized that her conversations with Father Pedro were not entirely spiritual. "I never thought that the great affection he

CONTINUED

bore me was wrong, although it could have been more pure. But there were also occasions on which, if we had not remained very much in God's presence, there would have been more serious offenses" (L 5.6).

Although Teresa is discreetly mute on the nature of her offenses with Father Pedro, her words imply that if their relationship had been somewhat different than it was, it could have led in the wrong direction. Relationships are paths that we walk; they take us in a direction for good or for ill. As John writes, "Love derived from sensuality terminates in sensuality, and the love that is of the spirit terminates in the spirit of God" (N 1.4.7).

Have you ever been in a relationship in which you asked yourself the question, "Where is this going; where will this end?"

NIGHT 1.5

Spiritual Anger

⌒◦◦⌒

John deals with three expressions of spiritual anger: first, anger as a reaction to a lack of consolation; second, anger at the imperfections of others; and third, anger toward oneself.

ANGER AS A REACTION TO A LACK OF CONSOLATION

> Because of the strong desire [*concupiscencia*] of many beginners for spiritual gratification, they usually have many imperfections of anger. When the delight and satisfaction procured in their spiritual exercises passes, these beginners are naturally left without any spiritual savor. And because of this distastefulness, they become peevish [*mala gracia*] in the works they do. (N 1.5.1)

This opening passage of chapter 5 is very similar to what John writes regarding spiritual avarice. "Many beginners also at times possess great spiritual avarice. They hardly ever seem content with the spirit God gives them. They become unhappy and peevish [*quejosos*] because they don't find the consolation they want in spiritual things" (N 1.3.1).

These two passages reveal a similarity between the spiritually angry and the spiritually avaricious. Both become distraught when they do not experience consolation. However, they are dissimilar in two significant ways. First, the strength of the desire for consolation between the spiritually angry and the spiritually avaricious is different. The intensity of desire for consolation in the spiritually angry is far greater than that of the spiritually avaricious. In writing of beginners possessed by spiritual anger, John uses a word for desire that he rarely uses in his writings—*concupiscencia*. Concupiscence, which is often connected with sexual desire, connotes a very, very strong desire.

The second difference between the spiritually angry and the spiritually avaricious follows from the first. Because the desire for consolation in the spiritually angry is far more intense than the desire for consolation in the spiritually avaricious, the reaction to being deprived of consolation is much more vehement in the former than in the latter. The spiritually avaricious become "peevish" (*quejosos*; N 1.3.1). *Quejosos* means to complain, to murmur, or to whine. However, the spiritually angry become "peevish" (*mala gracia*; N 1.5.1). *Mala gracia* literally means "bad grace," that is, their behavior toward others is graceless, rude, and boorish. "They are so unbearable [*no hay quien los sufra*] that nobody can put up with them" (N 1.5.1). *Sufra* means to suffer, to bear with patience or to tolerate. These beginners are *no sufra*, or as we would say in English, they are *insufferable*. In short, the anger that erupts and spews over in their behavior is often unbearable and intolerable.

ANGER AND DESIRE

Many things can provoke anger. They run the gamut from a normal reaction to an unexpected inconvenience and to righteous indignation that seeks to right wrongs and restore justice, as St. Thomas Aquinas teaches (*Summa Theologiae* [ST] I, II, q. 46, a. 7; II, II, q. 158, a. 8).[1]

However, all forms of anger, regardless of their cause, have one thing in common. They are reactions to frustrated desire, and the stronger the desire, the more violent the reaction when desire is frustrated. This is the first truth that John sets before us in this chapter. When an inordinate appetite or "strong desire [*concupiscencia*]" is frustrated, violent reactions can ensue, for it is often the case that "violent delights have violent ends." We can't judge to what extent the unbearable behavior of these beginners is sinful. However, John does seem to indicate that their conduct stems from an emotional immaturity due to a lack of impulse control, for they "are easily angered at the least thing" (N 1.5.1).

The reason John gives for this agitated state of mind is the contrast between the sensual consolation beginners experience in prayer and the lack of it outside of prayer. "This frequently occurs after they have experienced in prayer some recollection pleasant to the senses. After the delight and satisfaction are gone, the sensory part of the soul is left vapid [*desabrido*] and zestless" (N 1.5.1).

Desabrido refers to things that are insipid or tasteless. Thus, in contrast to the savor of consolation, everything else is experienced as being bland and drab. This is a common experience. How often has an exciting or relaxing weekend accentuated the dreariness of Monday morning? Who doesn't feel tired and wiped out when blindly groping to turn off the alarm clock? As adults, we heave a sigh, drag ourselves out of bed, crawl to the coffee maker, and get ready to meet the day's responsibilities. Peevish children react differently. They whine and throw a temper tantrum. The imperfection of spiritual anger is similar; it resides, not in feeling angry but in acting out upon the feeling of anger. The feeling does beginners no harm "if they do not allow this dejection to influence them" (N 1.5.1).

Here, John is setting before us another important truth. Regardless of the origin our feelings, they cannot harm us spiritually, if we accept God's grace not to act upon them. In fact, they can even be a source of virtue. Let's take an example from the life of St. Thérèse of Lisieux. Thérèse writes the following to her sister Céline: "What a grace when, in the morning, we feel no courage, no strength to practice virtue; that is the moment to put the axe to the root of the tree . . . and what a profit at the end of the day . . . in one act of love, even *unfelt* love, all is repaired" (L 1.467).

In short, it is precisely at those moments when we are devoid of consolation and feel desolate and disinclined to practice virtue that we are presented with the greatest opportunity to grow in virtue. This is because our love arises from the will alone, devoid of affective support—what Thérèse calls *unfelt* love.

ANGER AT OTHERS

Through a certain indiscreet [*desasosegado*] zeal they become angry over the sins of others, they reprove these others and sometimes even feel the impulse to do so angrily, which in fact they occasionally do, setting themselves up as lords [*dueños*] of virtue. (N 1.5.2)

A *dueño* is a proprietor or master of an estate. Thus, John compares these beginners to country squires who ride about their estates atop their high horses, overseeing the moral lives of others, and then become angry with "a certain indiscreet [*desasosegado*] zeal" when they spy some fault or imperfection. Within the context of this passage, *desasosegado* may best be translated as "being on the alert," for their zeal keeps tabs on what everyone is doing and not doing.

Similarly, St. Teresa warns us against "indiscreet [*indiscretos*] zeal" (IC 1.2.17). *Indiscretos* may be translated in various ways. However, within the context in which Teresa writes, it's best rendered as "intrusive," for she is dealing with nuns who possess "great zeal . . . [and] are careful to observe whether [others] commit [little faults] and then inform the prioress" (IC 1.2.17). In short, Teresa is writing about people who not merely see the faults of others but also are looking for them.

The question now arises, why are these beginners so intent on observing the faults of others? We do not know the source of their anger because John doesn't tell us. Perhaps it is pride. If we set ourselves up as the guardians of virtue and bastions of the standards of the community, then we can feel not only justified but also proud of our self-appointed role as the moral overseers of others.

Perhaps it is envy. It is sometimes the case that when we take a responsibility upon ourselves, we can become envious and resentful of others who do not feel the same obligation. Therefore, if we cannot lay down our self-imposed burden, we want others to suffer as we do. As C. S. Lewis puts it, "One of the marks of a certain type of bad man is that he cannot give up a thing himself without wanting everyone else to give it up."[2] How often do we attempt to force others to be as miserable as we have made ourselves?

But whatever the case may be, Teresa tells us that the consequences of observing the faults of others are destructive. First, such behavior can distort our perspective; things are blown out of proportion. "It could follow that every little fault the Sisters commit will seem to her a serious breach" (IC 1.2.16). Second, such a perspective makes a person vulnerable to the deceptions of the devil. "For when the devil tempts [us] through distress over the sins and failings of others . . . he puts it in [our] heads that this distress stems only from the desire that God not be offended and from concern for His honor. This desire disquiets [us] so much that it hinders [our] prayer; and the greatest harm lies in [us] thinking this distress amounts to virtue, perfection, and great zeal for God" (L 13.10).

Such blindness is frightening and can rob us of our humanity. As St. Francis de Sales writes, "We are sometimes so occupied with being good angels that we neglect to be good men and women."[3] When we believe that our zeal has divine approbation, what can we not do in the name of God? If we are on a crusade, armed with indiscreet zeal, we can do a great deal of damage. As Teresa told her nuns, "What the devil is hereby aiming after is no small thing: the cooling of charity and love the Sisters have for one another" (IC 1.2.17).

ANGER TOWARD SELF

Beginners become exasperated with themselves because they cannot accept the discrepancy between who they are and who they think they are. "In becoming aware of their own imperfections, [they] grow angry with themselves in unhumble impatience" (N 1.5.3). They increase their self-directed anger by "mak[ing] numerous plans and great resolutions" (N 1.5.3) that they don't have the capacity to fulfill. Having set the bar so high, they are bound to fail. As a result, they create a vicious cycle; the more they resolve to succeed, the more they fail. "The more resolves they make the more they break, and the greater becomes their anger" (N 1.5.3). Their pursuit of an imaginary perfection both creates and sustains their anger. As St. Francis de Sales writes, "For I am sure you will note that those interior troubles you have suffered have been caused by a great multitude of considerations and desires produced by an intense eagerness to attain some imaginary perfection. I mean that your imagination had formed for you an ideal of absolute perfection, to which your will wished to lift itself."[4]

The remedy, writes St. Francis, is the willingness to bear one's faults and failings with patient humility. "Those who aspire to the pure love of God have not so much need of patience with others as with themselves. We must suffer our imperfection in order to have perfection."[5]

MEEKNESS, THE ANTIDOTE OF ANGER

At the very end of this chapter, John mentions the remedial virtue to anger: meekness. "Their attitude is contrary to spiritual meekness and can only be remedied by the purgation of the dark night" (N 1.5.3). In this regard, John is following a tradition stretching from the ancient Greeks to Scholastic philosophy.

For Aristotle, meekness is the mean or midpoint between the two extremes of apathy and excessive anger. It is the virtue by which a person "gets angry at the right things and with the right people, and also in the right way and at the right time and for the right length of time."[6]

In the New Testament, the Greek words for meek (*praus*) and meekness (*praotēs*) refer to a beast that has been bridled;

they refer to passion that is under control. St. Thomas teaches that meekness is the strength that "restrains the onslaught of anger" (ST II, II, q. 157, a. 1) and "makes a man self-possessed" (ST II, II, q. 157, a. 4). It prevents a person from becoming dispossessed of his or her humanity in a swirl of anger.

Meekness is a part of temperance, the cardinal virtue that orders and harmonizes our passions and appetites with reason. Traditionally, temperance has been associated with aesthetics and beauty because it brings order, balance, and symmetry into our lives and safeguards us from engaging in irrational behavior.

It is very difficult to see ourselves when we are caught up in a swirl of anger. To do so, we need to stand outside ourselves, so to speak, and observe our behavior from a third-person omniscient point of view. In this regard, St. John Chrysostom makes the following suggestion.

> Will you learn what an evil is anger? Stand by while others are quarreling in the forum. In yourself you cannot easily see the disgrace of the thing, because your reason is darkened and drunken; but when you are clear from the passion, and while your judgment is sound, view your own case in others. Observe, I pray you, the crowds collecting round, and the angry men like maniacs acting shamefully in the midst. For when the passion boils up within the breast, and becomes excited and savage, the mouth breathes fire, the eyes emit fire, all the face becomes swollen, the hands are extended disorderly, the feet dance ridiculously, and they spring at those who restrain them, and differ nothing from madmen in their insensibility to all these things; nay, differ not from wild asses, kicking and biting. Truly a passionate man is not a graceful one.[7]

If we can view how ungraceful we become when we behave "like maniacs," the binding effect of shame can help to bridle our tongues. This is practicing meekness. As St. John Climacus writes, "The first step toward freedom from anger is to keep the lips silent when the heart is stirred . . . [so that] anger . . . [will] be restrained by the chains of meekness."[8]

However, this first step is not sufficient to expunge our wrath, for "an imperfection must be purged in . . . the dark night" (N 1.5.1). John's repeated insistence that all of the imperfections of beginners must be purged in the dark night is an important theological statement, namely, not that sin is weakness that can be overcome by human effort but that it can only be redeemed by God's grace. Nevertheless, our cooperation is a necessary step because the active night is the doorway into the passive night.

We need to keep in mind that the faults of beginners are manifestations of the capital sins. If these inclinations are indulged, they become stronger and express themselves in behavior that grows increasingly more violent. If they are resisted, we grow in meekness, the virtue of self-possession. If we are always losing our temper, the danger is that we can lose ourselves. Each of us must ask God to "set a guard over my mouth, O Lord: keep watch over the door of my lips" (Ps 141:3). "Then," writes St. Augustine, commenting upon this psalm, "the door will be a restraint for us, not our ruin."[9]

For Reflection

People who set themselves up as "lords of virtue" are harsh in their judgments of others. Their "indiscreet

CONTINUED

zeal" makes them vigilant regarding "the sins of others" (N 1.5.2). They are constantly on the lookout to find the mote in their brother's or sister's eye. This attitude is contrary to charity. As St. Augustine writes, "Just as severity is ready to punish the sins that it finds, so love does not want to find any to punish."[10]

Before beginners enter the dark night, they are haughty and judge others with severity. After they enter the dark night, "they . . . do not judge them as they did before. . . . [They] know only their own misery and keep it so much in sight that they have no opportunity to watch anyone else's conduct" (N 1.12.8).

To what extent do you keep watch over the conduct of others, ready to punish the sins that you find?

NIGHT 1.6

Spiritual Gluttony

～∽～

John's treatment of spiritual gluttons is similar to his treatment of the spiritually avaricious. Both are so attached to consolation that when they are deprived of it, they act like testy children. Yet, there is a difference. The spiritually avaricious are intent on acquisition, whereas spiritual gluttons crave experience. The former focus on accumulating knowledge and religious objects, but the latter "are attracted by the delight [*sabor*] they feel in their spiritual exercises" (N 1.6.1).

Another difference between the spiritually avaricious and spiritual gluttons is the type of pleasures they pursue. The former is of a more intellectual and aesthetic nature; the latter is more sensual. John describes the sensual nature of the pleasure that spiritual gluttons seek by repeating the word *sabor* that can be translated as taste, relish, or savor. They "strive for spiritual savor [*sabor*]" and are "attracted by the delight [*sabor*] they feel in their spiritual exercises" (N 1.6.1). They become addicted to "the sweetness" and "spiritual savor" of consolation (N 1.6.1) because they "experience intense satisfaction [*gran gusto*] in the performance of spiritual exercises" (N 1.1.2).

The *gran gusto*, the great pleasure, the intense satisfaction, or the enormous delight that these beginners experience can be so powerful and intoxicating that their judgment becomes darkened. The way they pursue these intense experiences can be frightening. They "go to extremes" to obtain it. "They kill themselves with penances, weaken themselves by fasts and . . . over tax their weakness" (N 1.6.1).

These beginners can become so addicted to consolation that "their only yearning and satisfaction is to do what they feel inclined to do" (N 1.6.2). They are so bent on their pursuit of consolation that they want no one to oppose them. This makes them both secretive and deceptive. They stealthily engage in spiritual practices "without counsel" (N 1.6.1) and "are guided . . . solely by their own opinion" (N 1.6.4), lest their lack of "discretion" (N 1.6.1) is discovered and they're told to either change or modify their behavior. If someone notices their behavior, they devise strategies that help them avoid change at all costs. "To avoid obedience they either add to, change, or modify what was commanded" (N 1.6.2).

Consider the following set of exchanges between a novice and his novice master. Since John was once a novice master (that is, one who was in charge of "beginners"), this example may not be far from his own experience.

Father John: Brother Pedro, there's something I need to talk to you about. I've heard that you're praying in the chapel late at night. Is this true?

Brother Pedro: Yes, Father John. God is blessing me with great consolation, and it's my great joy to render God thanks for the grace that he is bestowing upon me.

Father John: But you look really tired, and lately I've noticed you've fallen asleep several times during classes on the Rule.

Brother Pedro: You're right, Father John. But what's more important, prayer or study?

Father John: Both are important. However, you need to keep in mind, as I said in class, that prudence is the mother of all virtues. I want you to retire to your cell after Compline like the other novices.

Brother Pedro: Yes, Father John.

About a week later, Father John calls Brother Pedro into his office again.

Father John: Brother Pedro, what time do you go to bed, that is, what time do you go to sleep at night?

Brother Pedro: Why do you ask? I go to my cell after Compline as you told me to.

Father John: That is very commendable, but what time do you go to *sleep*?

Brother Pedro: That's hard to say. I pray in my cell as the Rule prescribes. (*Brother Pedro now quotes from the Carmelite Rule.*) "Each one of you is to stay in his own cell or nearby, pondering the Lord's law day and *night* and keeping watch at his prayers unless attending to some other duty."

Father John: Brother, I'm very aware of what our Rule says, and I am happy to know that you have made your cell a place of prayer. But there is another duty that you are obliged to fulfill in your cell—to get adequate sleep.

Brother Pedro: But our Holy Rule says we should meditate "day and *night!*"

Father John: Brother Pedro, I am very aware of what our Rule says, but I am telling you, as your novice master, that I want you to get more sleep. I'm beginning to find you somewhat disobedient.

Brother Pedro: Father John, I am *not* disobedient. I did *exactly* what you told me to do. I retired to my cell after Compline.

Father John: But when I told you to retire after Compline, you *knew* that I was telling you to get more sleep. We will talk about this later.

The above dialogue contains a sobering truth that applies to all of us, not just beginners. When we want something badly enough, we can become deceptive. We will find ways to circumvent any obstacle that stands in our path. We will invent reasons for which we can disregard legitimate authority, lay aside obligations, deceive others, and even act against our better judgment.

The psychological and spiritual dynamics of deceit and rationalization that John sets before us in this chapter are applicable to any inordinate desire. When we are blinded by desire, we desire to be blind, lest we see and be converted. Over time, our rationalizations can become so highly honed that we do not realize the change that is taking place within us. We become deceptive human beings.

When we first violate our conscience, we feel the pangs of regret. However, over time, we become hardened to its entreaties. We find an example of this in Robert Bolt's play *A Man for All Seasons*. In act 1, Cromwell tempts Richard Rich to betray Thomas More by offering him a lucrative job at court. Rich is torn. He is inordinately ambitious, yet he feels the sting of conscience in the prospect of betrayal. Unfortunately, ambition wins out. Rich gives Cromwell the information he wants.

Cromwell: There, that wasn't too painful, was it?

Rich: (*Laughing a little and a little rueful*) No!

Cromwell: That's all there is. And you'll find it easier next time.[1]

The poignancy of this exchange is twofold. First, in the very act of betrayal, Rich is painfully conscious of what he is doing. Ruefully, that is, with grief, regret, and sorrow, he betrays his friend. Second, as the play progresses, Cromwell's prediction comes true. Deceit and betrayal become easier and easier for Rich, until in the end he perjures himself. How does one come to such a pass? It happens gradually, one rationalization at a time.

PENANCES OF BEASTS

These beginners "go to extremes"; they "kill themselves with penances" in their inordinate pursuit of pleasure (N 1.6.1). Theirs is "a penance of beasts [because] . . . like beasts, they are motivated in these penances by an appetite for the pleasure they find in them" (N 1.6.2). To understand the connection between pleasure and excessive penances, let us consider two examples that were common in John's day: the discipline and excessive fasting.

THE DISCIPLINE

The discipline is a whip of cords or chains that was commonly used by monks and nuns to scourge themselves either in remembrance of Christ's scourging or in reparation for sins committed. Though "taking the discipline" was usually used within the bounds of reason and moderation, it was sometimes used to excess. It is the excess of spiritual gluttons that

John condemns, those who "go to extremes and pass beyond the mean in which virtue resides" (N 1.6.1).

Why would spiritual gluttons inflict pain upon themselves in order to obtain pleasure? One explanation is that the excitation of pain and pleasure are closely connected. Physiologists have discovered that one of the effects of pain is the production of natural endorphins that trigger a "high" comparable to what is experienced during intense physical exercise. Since spiritual gluttons desire an intense experience, it would naturally follow that they would go to extremes in inflicting pain upon themselves.

The problem of "taking the discipline," of engaging in this "penance of beasts" may seem irrelevant in our own day. However, we should not rush to judgment, for there are two prominent factors in our culture that can contribute to such masochistic behavior. The first is the prevalence of borderline disorders, a common feature of which is self-mutilating behavior as a way to combat emotional numbness. The second factor is that many young people today are attracted to traditional forms of asceticism. Combine these two factors in an individual with an inordinate attachment to consolation. Do you understand where there may be a problem?

EXCESSIVE FASTING

St. Teresa writes of individuals who are so attached to the consolation that accompanies the prayer of quiet that in order to both heighten and prolong the pleasurable experience, they engage in extreme fasting, which can produce a dreamy state of consciousness. Teresa's advice to prioresses regarding such nuns absorbed in this self-induced state of peaceful languor was to "take away the fasts and disciplines" (F 6.5). In his treatment of spiritual gluttons, John is dealing with the same dynamic. "They weaken themselves by fasts" because "they are motivated in these penances by an appetite for the pleasure they find in them" (N 1.6.1–2).

Regardless of the type of penance that is practiced by spiritual gluttons, the pleasure they derive from them is so delightful that their insistence that they be allowed to continue to perform their penances is frightening. They "are [so] insistent [*porfiados*] that their spiritual directors allow them to do what they want . . . [that they] almost force permission" (N 1.6.3).

Porfiados means not just insistent but also persistent. It is their repeated incessant demands that almost force their directors to give permission. It is easy to imagine their directors throwing up their hands in exasperation and saying, "Okay, then do what you want!"

OBSTINACY

One of the great dangers of being persistently "unreasonable" and insistent on "doing [one's] own will" (N 1.6.2) is that winning, per se, gradually becomes more important than the object one is fighting for. John hints at this phenomenon when he says these beginners can become so oppositional in the face of authority and so insistent on getting their way that they refuse to do something merely because they are told to do so, even if they want to do what they are commanded. "Any obedience in this matter is distasteful to them. Some reach such a point that the mere obligation of obedience to perform their spiritual exercises makes them lose all desire and devotion. Their only yearning and satisfaction is to do what they feel inclined to do." (N 1.6.2)

When our satisfaction becomes fused with getting our own way, we become inclined to be obstinate because we derive joy from the feeling of triumph. As Aristotle writes regarding obstinate people, "They delight in the victory they gain if they are not persuaded to change."[2]

They regard not being able to be moved as a sign of strength, which becomes a source of pride. As St. Thomas writes, an obstinate person holds "to his own opinion because he wishes by doing so to show off his own excellence" (ST II, II, q. 138, a. 2). However, such people are incapable of seeing that their obstinate attachment to winning makes them a slave to it. As Alexander Pope so rightly said, "An obstinate man does not hold opinions, but they hold him."

DESIRE AND JUDGMENT

We all know that strong emotions can cloud our judgment. For example, when we are blinded by rage, we may make decisions against our own self-interest. Fortunately, fits of anger are usually bouts of temporary insanity. When we calm down, our judgment is restored.

John is concerned with not a temporary loss of judgment due to emotions, which are often beyond our control, but a permanent loss of judgment that is rooted in the will. In this chapter, John draws our attention to one of the greatest harms that result from having an inordinate attachment to consolation. A faulty criterion is formed for evaluating and judging what is and what is not spiritual. These beginners use an emotional yardstick for judging the spiritual worth of what they do to such an extent that "if they do not procure any sensible feeling and satisfaction, they think they have accomplished nothing. As a result they judge poorly . . . and think that they have done nothing" (N 1.6.5–6).

So far, John has helped us to interpret emotional experience from a spiritual perspective. These beginners interpret spiritual experience from an emotional perspective. Since their whole basis of evaluating their spiritual life and their self-worth is an emotional barometer, they are "always hunting for some gratification in the things of God" (N 1.6.6). For example, "in receiving Communion they spend all their time trying to get some feeling and satisfaction rather than humbly praising and reverencing God dwelling within them" (N 1.6.5).

The effort these individuals expend in trying to extract some feeling from the reception of the Eucharist reinforces their faulty judgment. It prevents them from seeing why God withholds consolation from them. "God often withdraws sensory delight and pleasure so that souls might set the eyes of faith on this invisible grace" (N 1.6.5). How different their attitude toward consolation and understanding the ways of God is compared to that of St. Thérèse. "I can't say that I frequently received consolations when making my thanksgivings after Mass; perhaps it is the time when I receive the least. However, I find this very understandable since I have offered myself to Jesus not as one desirous of her own consolation in His visit but simply to please Him who is giving Himself to me" (S 172).

The greatest danger that John foresees for people who "judge very poorly" (N 1.6.5) the ways of God is that they will become spiritual directors and perpetuate their faulty judgment. These "directors will tell [their directees] that they are falling back since they find no satisfaction or consolation . . . in the things of God" (A Prol 5). Therefore, John warns us to "take care into whose hands [we] entrust [ourselves], for the disciple will become like the master, as is the father so will be the son" (F 3.30).

For Reflection

At the beginning of *Romeo and Juliet*, Romeo is madly in love with Rosaline, whom he considers the most beautiful woman since time began. "The all-seeing Sun / never saw her Match since first the World begun" (act 1, scene 2, lines 95–96). However, that evening, when Romeo crashes a party at the Capulets, Rosaline's beauty is outshone when he sets his eyes upon Juliet. "Did my Heart love till now? . . . For I ne'er saw true Beauty till this Night" (act 1, scene 4, line 167).

The next day when Romeo tells Friar Lawrence of his undying love for Juliet, Lawrence responds,

> Holy Saint Francis, what a Change is here!
> Is Rosaline, that thou didst love so dear,
> So soon forsaken? Young Men's Love then lies
> Not truly in their Hearts but in their Eyes.
>
> (act 2, scene 2, lines 64–68)

Romeo rejects what Friar Lawrence says because he believes the measure of true love is determined by the intensity of emotion. If *Romeo and Juliet* had ended with this pair of star-crossed lovers riding off happily into the sunset, one wonders how long their life

CONTINUED

together would have lasted? When Romeo's intense feelings for Juliet had subsided, might he not seek out another experience? Just as Augustine said of his youth, "I was in love with love,"[3] so too was Romeo in love with the experience of being in love.

The beginners that John describes in this chapter are like Romeo. Just as he is in love not with a woman but with the intoxication that physical beauty excites within him, so too are these beginners in love not with God but with the intoxicating consolations of God. In consequence, they are "always hunting for some gratification in the things of God" (N 1.6.6) and forever "seeking after these delights" (N 1.6.1).

These beginners are like blind adolescents who equate love with the intensity of their feelings. "They judge very poorly" (N 1.6.5); they judge the depth of their spiritual lives with an emotional yardstick. "They think the whole matter of prayer consists in looking for sensory satisfaction and devotion" (N 1.6.6).

If Romeo is to grow up, he will have to judge the true nature of love, which consists in not feelings but the willingness to sacrifice for one's beloved. So too if beginners are to "be purged of [their] childishness" (N 1.6.6), it is necessary for them to tread "the rough way of the cross" (N 1.6.7) and realize that the "value of their works do not depend . . . on the satisfaction found in them but on knowing how to practice self-denial in them" (N 1.6.8).

CONTINUED

Human nature being what it is, you will always want to experience the consolations of God, but how much do you seek them? Do you judge your state of soul based upon the satisfaction that you find in your spiritual exercises, or have you come to realize that the rough way of the cross is the only path to holiness?

NIGHT 1.7

Spiritual Envy and Sloth

〜⌒〜

Everything that John has written regarding the faults of beginners falls under two categories. The first is pride, whereby beginners interpret the experience of consolation from a narcissistic perspective. The second is sensuality, whereby beginners have an insatiable thirst for the sensual gratification of consolation. It is within this perspective that we can understand why John chose to deal with both envy and sloth last. Envy and sloth (*acedia*) are pride and sensuality that have come to full term; they are the chief characteristics of a person in whom love has grown cold.

The Sadness of Envy

There are many emotions connected to envy: fear, desire, anger, joy, and sorrow. The envious fear anyone who competes with them for the limelight, so they often discredit their rivals. "They cannot bear to hear others being praised without contradicting and undoing these compliments as much as possible" (N 1.7.1). And if their attempts to discredit are unsuccessful, "their annoyance grows because they themselves do not receive these plaudits" (N 1.7.1).

In addition, the envious find delight in the misfortunes of others and grieve in the face of another's joy. "[They] feel sad about the spiritual good of others and experience sensible grief [*pena*] in noting that their neighbor is ahead of them on the road to perfection. . . . Learning of the virtues of others makes them sad" (N 1.7.1). Grief is a good translation of *pena*, for besides sorrow, *pena* includes the feelings of affliction, anxiety, and agitation. In short, envy exhibits many of the symptoms of depression.

Envy is a depressive sadness and a twofold grief. First, it is a grief of the ego, which mourns its dreams to be praised and held in esteem above all others. Second, envy is a sadness of soul, an inability to find joy in the happiness of others. Envy can so deform us that we can only find happiness in the misfortunes of others. As one soul on the cornice of envy in Dante's *Purgatorio* says, "I found more joy in the bad luck of others than in the good that fell to my own lot."[1] If envy is permitted to grow, it can so ulcerate the soul that bitterness, resentment, and spite will become its very life. These people bear a grudge against happiness itself.

We have an example of this state of soul in the character of Hippolyte in Dostoyevsky's novel *The Idiot*. Hippolyte is a young man dying of tuberculosis. He has grown bitter on life. He is angry at the injustice of the world and is resentful that he has been deprived of the happiness that he sees in the lives of others. On his deathbed, he has a private conversation with Prince Myshkin, a kind man who has taken him into his care. Myshkin is engaged to a beautiful young woman named Aglaya Epanchina. Hippolyte had expressed his love to her, but she had rejected him in favor of Myshkin. In their conversation, Hippolyte asks Myshkin what he must do to die a peaceful death. "'I see I must make arrangements to die soon. . . . Before you go, just give me your opinion: how do you think I ought to die? I mean, the best, the most virtuous way? Tell me!' 'You should pass us by and forgive us our happiness,' said the prince in a low voice."[2]

We envy people many things: their beauty, their health, their possessions, their education, their success, their marriage, their children, their reputation, their goodness. However, in reality, we envy people only one thing: their happiness. Forgiving people their happiness is the only way out of misery.

JOHN'S TREATMENT OF ENVY

John's treatment of envy cannot be understood in isolation. It needs to be read in relationship to his treatment on pride because envy is not merely an emotion. It is an interpersonal relationship between ourselves and the gifts and talents of others. This is why proud beginners want "others to recognize their spirit and devotion" (N 1.2.3) and "cannot bear to hear others praised" (N 1.7.1).

Envy, like pride, is competitive because it is comparative by nature. The envious person does not desire to be beautiful, intelligent, talented, rich, or holy; rather, he or she seeks to be more beautiful, more intelligent, more talented, richer, or holier than others. In consequence, a beginner's pride is bruised when someone else seizes the limelight. John's focus in his treatment on envy is on two reactions to wounded pride: sadness and anger. To understand these reactions, let us explore them within the framework of narcissism.

The self-esteem of narcissists is fragile and in need of constant affirmation. When narcissists don't receive the admiration or affirmation that they desperately crave, they will either spiral downward into depression or fly into a rage. Take the example of an author who feels that he has written the Great American Novel. If, after it has been published for only a month, he doesn't receive a call from the Nobel Prize committee, one of two things is likely to occur. He will either become deflated because he hasn't received the recognition and acclaim that he had fantasized or become enraged at those idiots and dolts in Sweden because they don't have the brains to recognize his greatness.

The first reaction is directed inward; the second reaction is directed outward. John describes a similar dynamic. When attention is diverted from the proud beginner to someone else, his ego receives a blow. He will either sink into "sensible grief" (N 1.7.1) or, out of livid envy, try to destroy his rival's reputation. It is worth noting that the specific tactics that these beginners use to destroy their neighbor's good name are devious—"contradicting [*contrario*] and undoing [*deshaciendo*] . . . compliments" (N 1.7.1). Both words have sinister connotations attached to them. *Contrario* can mean to contradict or to negate what is being asserted with a hurtful and even mischievous motive. Likewise, *deshaciendo*, derived from *deshacer*, can mean to diminish, to cancel out, and even to destroy. Notice that neither contradicting nor undoing is a frontal attack. Neither says anything that is negative against one's opponent. They simply negate and cancel out the good.

The envious are dissemblers. They sow seeds of suspicion in the minds of others under the guise of concern and caution. For example, they may say something like, "Yes, what you say is true. Brother Thaddeus is a good man, but there is something about him that makes me feel uncomfortable." Once the envious person has covered his devious tracks by asserting the goodness of Brother Thaddeus, he negates and cancels out what he has said by insinuating that Brother Thaddeus may not be the person he appears to be.

The envious are sly hypocrites; they mask their evil under the cloak of goodness. The poison that they secrete is insidious because it is invisible. In *Paradise Lost*, Satan comes to Earth out of envious spite to corrupt Adam and Eve. To accomplish his end, Satan disguises himself as an innocent cherub in order to deceive the angel Uriel, Earth's sentinel. Satan's words are spoken with such disarming innocence that Uriel is deceived. In consequence, he allows Satan admittance to earth. John Milton's commentary on this encounter is as follows: "So spake the false dissembler unperceived, for neither man nor angel can discern Hypocrisy, the only evil that walks Invisible, except to God alone" (book 3, 680–84).

The corrosiveness of envy becomes visible to beginners when God places them in the dark night. Grace makes them "aware of how miserable they are" (N 1.13.8). This misery is graphically described by St. Cyprian in his work "Jealousy and Envy." "Of such a sort, indeed, is the gnawing worm of the soul. What a plague on one's thought [is envy]. To turn the good things of another to one's own evil . . . to be tormented by the prosperity of [others], to make the glory of others one's own punishment."[3]

When we are submerged in the dark night, even our torment is transformed by grace. It becomes increasingly more painful to spew out the poison of envy, for in doing so, we are left with a bitter aftertaste in our mouth. This is an experience of grace that acts as a restraining force.

Charity, which has been traditionally regarded as the virtue that opposes envy, takes the form of restraint. In this regard, John writes of the benefit of the dark night in conjunction with envy. "As for envy, these individuals also become charitable toward others. For if they do have envy, it will not be vicious as before" (N 1.13.8).

It is important to note what John is and is not saying in this passage. By connecting "becom[ing] charitable" with "not be[ing] vicious," John is saying that the grace of the dark night gives these envious souls the strength to struggle to restrain their tongues, so that they will not spew out vicious words upon the world. "I will guard my ways that I may not sin with my tongue; I will keep a muzzle on my mouth" (Ps 39:1).

However, John does not say that the capital sin of envy, that is, the inclination to mouth vicious words, is eradicated. Rather, the grace of restraint is given to bridle the inclination. When God places us in the dark night, "envy [that is, the capital sin of envy] . . . will not be vicious as before" (N 1.13.8).

Grace may or may not heal the inclination of envy. But even if it is not healed, the inclination is no longer an obstacle to spiritual growth. This is because the ultimate goal of life that John sets before us is union with God, which is a union of wills. If you are struggling to muzzle your mouth, then you are growing in the love of God and love of neighbor.

THE SADNESS OF SLOTH

John tells us that the most damaging consequence of being so "inclined toward [sensual] delights" is that it makes one "weak and remiss in treading the rough way of the cross. A soul given up to pleasure naturally feels aversion toward the bitterness of self-denial" (N 1.6.7). When this inclination toward pleasure and its aversion to exert effort comes to full term, we are dealing with sloth or *acedia*.

Of all the capital sins, *acedia* is the most subtle, complex, and difficult to define. It is not mere indolence, though

lethargy is one of its characteristics; it is a sluggish indiffer-
ence, a joyless self-seeking, and an agitated sadness. At one
moment, *acedia* makes us crave the company of others as a
relief from the burden of self; the next moment we are so upset
with people that we cannot be civil to anyone.

It is a sullen restlessness in which we sink into a black hole
of dejection and explode into an ill-tempered rage. It is filled
with both crippling lassitude and restless agitation. It vacillates
between ennui and boredom; "it either learns to succumb to
sleep or shakes off its restraints of the cell . . . and gets into
the habit of . . . visiting a brother," writes John Cassian.[4]
Acedia exhibits all the symptoms of depression in both its veg-
etative and agitated forms because *acedia* is a type of depression. It is a depression of the spirit; it is a loss of self. It is a
state of a soul that has given up the spiritual quest yet retains
and mourns its desire for God.

As both an affective state and inclination, *acedia* is not
a sin for it "is found in holy men" (ST II, II q. 35, a. 3). It
is only when we freely *consent* to the mood of *acedia* that we
become culpable. As a choice, *acedia* is a flight from self, a
withdrawal from the demands of charity and all that pertains to doing God's will; it is "an aversion from the Divine
good" (Thomas Aquinas, ST II, II, q. 35, a. 3). In consequence, since "the primary effect of charity is joy in God"
(ST II, II, q. 35, a. 3), the more we choose to succumb
to the mood of *acedia*, the more we withdraw from the
source of our happiness and sink deeper and deeper into
depressive sadness.

The sinking sadness of *acedia* is like a backward glance
upon "what might have been." A person sunk in *acedia* experiences one's desire for God as a memory "that it was happy
once upon a time," as St. Augustine puts it.[5] *Acedia* is the note

of eternal sorrow that St. Thomas Aquinas says borders upon the brink of "despair" (ST II, II, q. 35, a. 4). It is the soul's sadness in the face of its own good, just as envy is sadness in the face of its neighbor's good.

When we are mired down in *acedia*, we are tempted to give up the spiritual quest. Life becomes tedious and empty of meaning, and we seriously doubt whether we will ever be happy again. In such a state of soul, we begin to settle for the relief of an effortless existence that shrivels our capacity to exert effort. We can be brought to the brink of despair, conscious that we have sunken into the slough of despond and do not feel the strength to extricate ourselves from it.

Now that we have a working knowledge of the capital sin of sloth (*acedia*), let us now turn to John's treatment of *acedia*.

> Also regarding spiritual sloth [*acidia espiritual*], these beginners usually become weary [*tedio*] in exercises that are more spiritual and flee from them since these exercises are contrary to sensory satisfaction. Since they are so used to finding delight in spiritual practices, they become bored when they do not find it. If they do not receive in prayer the satisfaction they crave—for after all it is fit that God withdraw this so as to try them—they do not want to return to it, or at times they either give up prayer or go to it begrudgingly. (N 1.7.2)

Since John is dealing with *acedia* in beginners, he does not present it in its final stage, as we have outlined above, but in its incipient form. They have not given up the spiritual quest, but they are beginning to avoid it. They are torn. They want to avoid any spiritual exercise or act of charity that they find boring or tedious but feel guilty for doing so. For example, they flee from prayer because it does not provide them with the sensory satisfaction that they crave but often return to it against their will. "They do not want to return to [prayer]" but do so "begrudgingly" (N 1.7.2).

These beginners respond to the demands of the spiritual life grudgingly because they are at odds with their ruling desire: freedom. "They expect to go about in spiritual matters according to the whims [*a sus anchuras*] and satisfactions of their own will." *A sus anchuras* can be translated as "at full liberty" or "at large."

In short, they want the freedom to do whatever they please; they do not want any strictures placed upon their lives that would tie them down to a boring existence. In this regard, "whim" is a good translation of the Spanish *a sus anchuras* because it captures the mercurial character of *acedia* that constantly changes direction to avoid anything unpleasant.

However, as they flee, these beginners *know* that they are relinquishing the source of their joy. "They become sad if they have to desire God's will" (N 1.7.3). Thus, these beginners find themselves trapped between sadness and sadness. They feel a sinking sadness that drains all their energy as they approach doing something unpleasant. However, as they avoid doing God's will, they feel a depressive sadness as they mourn the source of their happiness. They try to resolve this spiritual conflict with a psychological solution. They fashion God in their own image and likeness. "They frequently believe that what is not their will, or brings them no satisfaction, is not God's will, and, on the other hand, that if they are satisfied, God is too. They measure God by themselves and not themselves by God" (N 1.7.3).

Since "they become weary in exercises that are more spiritual . . . and become sad if they have to desire to do God's will" (N 1.7.2–3), they need to convince themselves that such practices are not of God. It is easy to imagine a beginner arguing as follows: "Since joy and peace are fruits of the spirit and lackluster spiritual exercises and mundane duties make me depressed, they cannot be part of God's design but rather are expressions of an outmoded masochistic spirituality." These beginners believe that the imposition of restrictions causes them to be depressed. However, the problem is that they are either unable or unwilling to distinguish between two similar but very different forms of grief, namely, mourning and depression.

Sigmund Freud's monograph *Mourning and Melancholia* contains a psychological distinction between mourning and depression, which can help us to understand the basic choice that confronts beginners struggling against *acedia*.

Mourning (uncomplicated or normal grief) and melancholia (clinical depression) often share a common cause: a loss. However, what differentiates one from the other, says Freud, is how a person reacts to the loss. In the face of loss, our initial response is to resist and deny that a love object has been taken away from us. However, over time, a critical choice has to be made. If we can accept the reality of loss, then we enter into the painful, healing process of mourning. However, if we are unable to internally let go of what has been taken away from us, we will sink into melancholia. In mourning, we "withdraw . . . libido from the [lost loved] object . . . [whereas in melancholia we] "withdraw into the ego."[6] Similarly, beginners who cannot mourn when God withdraws from them "the breasts of these gratifications and delights" (N 1.7.5) withdraw from life by "run[ning] sadly from everything rough" (N 1.7.4). They fail to grasp that "entering the narrow way of life . . . is saddening" (N 1.7.4) not because it makes one depressed but because it involves mourning. The tragic irony of these beginners is that the more that they avoid mourning what the spiritual life entails, the more depressed they become.

These beginners are faced with a dilemma. They want to avoid everything that is difficult or demanding, but they cannot completely withdraw from life. They want to avoid carrying the cross, but they also want to do God's will. This ambivalence is manifested in their prayer. Sometimes they are faithful, and sometimes they are not. "They do not want to return to [prayer] or at times they either give up prayer or go to it begrudgingly" (N 1.7.2). Because they do things unwillingly, they do not carry their cross. They drag it.

Slothful people drag themselves through life because they are unable or unwilling to fully engage in life. We have an example of this in Anton Chekhov's play *The Three Sisters* where Irina, a very indolent and bored woman, comes to believe that the reason she is bored is because she is idle and that the antidote for her boredom is to work. Therefore, she obtains employment at the local telegraph office. One night, Irina comes home from work, sits down upon the couch wearily, and says with irritation, "A lady came to telegraph her brother in Saratov, that her son had died today, and she couldn't remember the address. So she sent it without an address, simply to Saratov. She was crying. And I was rude to her, for no reason whatever. And I said to her, 'I haven't got the time.' I must look for another job, this one is not right for me. What I want, what I dream of, is the very thing that's lacking. This work is without meaning because it lacks poetry."[7]

Irina quit her job not because it lacked poetry but because she lacked the capacity to bear the burden of the prose of daily life. The grief-stricken woman presented Irina with an opportunity to engage deeply in life; however, she didn't have the capacity to recognize it.

Boredom is a symptom of being disengaged from life. Its antidote, prescribed by the desert writers, is to embrace the ordinariness of life, not to flee from it. "Entering the narrow way of life" (N 1.7.4) is to focus on the life that God sets before us. The paradox of charity is that it does not constrict our life but expands our soul. One might think otherwise, since charity demands that we attend to the concrete realities in time and space. Charity is the mystery of the Incarnation, an encounter with the person of Christ becoming incarnate in our lives. It is "the point of intersection of the timeless with time, an occupation for the saint."[8]

Conversely, the more we "run sadly from everything that is rough" (N 1.7.4) and flee from the tedious demands of charity, the more our will becomes constricted and we become imprisoned within the narrow circumference of our moods and feelings.

Wallace Stevens's poem "The Dwarf" captures the final state of *acedia*, a person who has become wintered, constricted, and straitjacketed in his or her response to God and neighbor. "Now it is September and the web is woven . . . and you have to wear it. The winter is made and you have to bear it. . . . The winter web . . . is all that you are, the final dwarf of you."[9]

Stevens's poem contains a sobering truth. What we become is not an accident. It is woven and made. The strictures of our will are the results of our choices. The despair of *acedia* becomes manifest in the moment when we desire to love but realize that we have lost the ability to do so. This is graphically portrayed in Charles Dickens's story *A Christmas Carol*, as Marley's ghost departs.

Scrooge followed to the window: desperate in his curiosity. He looked out. The air was filled with phantoms, wandering hither and thither in restless haste, and moaning as they went. Every one of them wore chains like Marley's Ghost; some few (they might be guilty governments) were linked together; none were free. Many had been personally known to Scrooge in their lives. He had been quite familiar with one old ghost, in a white waistcoat, with a monstrous iron safe attached to its ankle, who cried piteously at being unable to assist a wretched woman with an infant, whom it saw below, upon a door-step. The misery with them all was, clearly, that they sought to interfere, for good, in human matters, and had lost the power forever.[10]

Acedia and envy bring misery into our lives. They deprive us of the power to love. They seal up in our souls the wellspring of divine joy and make us barren. Can there be any greater incentive to enter the dark night than to be purified of the source of our misery and to regain our happiness?

For Reflection

The target of envy's attack is not one's doing but one's being. Cinderella, for example, owns nothing but her work and the attitude with which she approaches it. But her sisters envy her. . . . Seated in her ashes, going cheerfully about her duties, dressed in rags, the suffering servant has an unmistakable lure about her that the envious sisters clearly lack.[11]

CONTINUED

This passage from *Cinderella and Her Sisters: The Envied and the Envying* by Ann and Barry Ulanov captures the essence of spiritual envy. The spiritually envious feel a lack of something they cannot have, a quality of being that they feel they cannot acquire. Spiritual envy does not envy any particular gift or talent that another person has; rather, it envies who a person has *become* as a result of grace.

The spiritually envious are consumed by impotent rage. The feel they cannot acquire what the envied persons possess, so they try to diminish their reputation in the minds of others. "They cannot bear to hear others being praised without contradicting and undoing these compliments as much as possible" (N 1.7.1).

There is a tragic irony in spiritual envy. The spiritually envious feel "sensible grief in noting that their neighbor is ahead of them"; however, they fall further behind their neighbor when they engage in envious behavior (N 1.7.1). This is because such behavior is "contrary to charity" (N 1.7.1), the very life of God.

How do you stop envying the person who is "ahead" of you because God has showered that person with more graces than he has you? St. Thérèse struggled with this question. She "wondered . . . why all souls don't receive an equal amount of graces" (S 13). She arrived at the following answer.

> [Jesus] set before me the book of nature; I understood how all the flowers He created are beautiful,

CONTINUED

how the splendor of the rose and whiteness of the Lily do not take away the perfume of the little violet or the delightful simplicity of the daisy. I understood that if all flowers wanted to be roses, nature would lose her springtime beauty, and the fields would no longer be decked out with little wild flowers.

And so it is in the world of souls, Jesus' garden. He willed to create great souls comparable to Lilies and roses, but He has created smaller ones and these must be content to be daisies or violets destined to give joy to God's glances when He Looks down at his feet. Perfection consists in doing His will, in being what He wills us to be. (S 13–14)

Can you be content with the person that God has willed you to be? It is the only way to true peace.

Frederick Faber, in his conference titled "The Monotony of Piety," writes that "the three leading characteristics of the spiritual life must always be effort, detail and slowness [that produce] . . . an insufferable monotony."[12] These words describe the challenge of living an authentic spiritual life—to fight against the same temptations and to struggle to love the same people day in and day out. The willingness to bear the insufferable monotony of the obligations of daily life is the antidote to *acedia*. Where in your life do you "run sadly from everything rough" (N 1.7.4)? Where in your life do you embrace the prose of life?

THE REMEMBRANCE OF PAST GRACES

As we come to the end of John's treatment of beginners, let us explore the following question: after consolation is withdrawn from the beginner, does it cease to exist in the soul, or does it continue to serve a purpose on the spiritual path? John would affirm the latter, for he teaches that a grace received in the past is operative in the memory.

> Only for the sake of moving the spirit to love should the soul at times recall the images and apprehensions that produced love. The effect produced by the remembrance of this communication is not as strong as the effect at the time the communication was received, yet when the communication is recalled there is a renewal of love and an elevation of the mind to God. This is especially true when the soul remembers some figures, images, or supernatural feelings. These are usually so imprinted on it that they last a long time; some are never erased from the soul. These apprehensions produce, almost as often as remembered, divine effects of love, sweetness, light, and so on—sometimes in a greater degree, sometimes in a lesser—because God impressed them for this reason. This is consequently a great grace, for those on whom God bestows it possess within themselves a mine of blessings. (A 3.13.6)

The graces of consolation that are recorded in memory are fused with the contexts in which they were originally experienced, that is, the "figures, images, or supernatural feelings" (A 3.13.6). Consequently, when the figures, images, or supernatural feelings that surrounded an experience of consolation are called to mind, we reexperience the grace that was communicated to us.

Take the example of a beginner who was frequently showered with consolation in a specific chapel when she was praying. She can no longer pray in this chapel, since she's moved away from the area where it is located. Still, during times of prayer, she often calls the chapel to mind. Mentally, she places herself in the chapel. By doing so, her mind becomes focused, and she feels drawn into the presence of God. The past graces of consolation recorded in her memory have become an inner sanctuary, a "mine of blessings" (A 3.13.6) that continues to nourish her soul.

What John teaches regarding graces received in the past that are operative in the memory is not restricted to experiences that are explicitly religious, for God's grace is communicated to us in various ways. Let us consider the following example.

In 1798, after an absence of five years, William Wordsworth revisited the ruins of Tintern Abbey situated in the picturesque Wye Valley in Wales. During his visit, he wrote his now-famous poem "Lines written a few miles above Tintern Abbey." The poem, though it begins by describing the landscape of the Welsh countryside, is primarily about the landscape of memory. It recounts how in the five intervening years between his first and second visit to the Wye Valley, the "beauteous forms" stored in memory, what John calls "figures, images, or supernatural feelings," had been a source of spiritual nourishment that provided "tranquil restoration" to his mind and influenced his deeds of kindness.

These beauteous forms,
Through a long absence, have not been to me
As is a landscape to a blind man's eye:
But oft, in lonely rooms, and 'mid the din

Of towns and cities, I have owed to them
In hours of weariness, sensations sweet,
Felt in the blood, and felt along the heart;
And passing even into my purer mind,
With tranquil restoration: —feelings too
Of unremembered pleasure: such, perhaps,
As have no slight or trivial influence
On that best portion of a good man's life,
His little, nameless, unremembered, acts
Of kindness and of love.[13]

For Wordsworth, the beauty of the Wye Valley was a grace recorded in his memory that, when recalled to mind, had a salutary effect upon his life—"a renewal of love and an elevation of the mind to God" (A 3.13.6).

For Reflection

St. Augustine writes that "in the fields and vast caverns of memory . . . you [my God] have dwelt . . . ever since I learned to know you, and it is there that I find you."[14]

In what fields or vast caverns in your memory does God dwell?

Do you realize that you "possess within [yourself] a mine of blessings" (A 3.13.6)?

NIGHT 1.8

The End of John's Consideration
of Beginners

~~~∽⌒∽~~~

I n this short chapter, John ends his consideration of beginners as he describes how God weans them away from consolation and brings them into the passive night of sense in
order to purify them of their attachments to sense and ego.
However, we need to remember that the underlying causes
of the imperfections of beginners, the capital sins, vary in
degree from person to person. Thus, even though John
is confident that "the majority of them do enter [the dark
night]" (N 1.8.4), we should not presuppose that all beginners will be able to do so. Some may turn back on the spiritual road, for "they do not want to enter the dark night or
allow themselves to be placed in it" (A Prol 3). When this
is the case, the inclinations of the capital sins will reattach
themselves to the objects of this world.

However, there are other beginners in whom consolation
has accomplished the twofold task for which it was given.
First, consolation has begun to wean them away from earthly
attachments. Second, during the time of consolation, these
beginners have begun to practice virtue and establish good
habits of prayer. "For it is through the delight and satisfaction

they experience in prayer that they have become detached from worldly things and have gained some spiritual strength in God. This strength has helped them somewhat to restrain their appetites for creatures, and through it they will be able to suffer a little oppression without turning back" (N 1.8.3). As this passage indicates, the strength that has been gained during the period of consolation is rudimentary. As John puts it, they have "gained some spiritual strength," which has "helped them somewhat to restrain their appetites for creatures." Nevertheless, John believes that the strength that has been acquired is adequate for these beginners "to suffer a little oppression and dryness without turning back" (N 1.8.3). It is these people with whom John will deal for the rest of his treatment of the dark night.

The dark night is composed of two purgations that correspond to the two parts of the soul: sense and spirit. The first purgation, the night of sense, accommodates sense to spirit and is the common condition of many, whereas the second night, the night of the spirit, is a more radical purification and "is the lot of the very few" (N 1.8.1).

In the next chapter, John will begin his treatment of those who enter the night of sense, where God withdraws his consoling presence from them. However, this does not mean that God has withdrawn; rather, the mode of the inflow of God has changed from consolation to contemplation. This means that the dark night is not devoid of God's presence. "This night . . . *is* contemplation" (N 1.8.1; italics added). As we continue, we must always keep in mind that the dark night *is* the work of grace. It "is an inflow of God into the soul" (N 2.5.1).

For Reflection

When God withdraws consolation from beginners, "in their opinion . . . everything seems to be functioning in reverse" (N 1.8.3). This is because they measure the depth of their spiritual life with an emotional yardstick. However, in reality, they are not regressing but progressing on the spiritual road. As God "withdraw[s] them from this base manner of loving," he is "lead[ing] them to a higher degree of divine love" (N 1.8.3). In short, God gives them the grace to love without the support of emotion.

Have you ever felt that you were regressing on the spiritual path because your prayer felt dry?

When prayer is dry, do you realize that God is giving you the strength to walk the desert road of genuine love?

The Withdrawal of Consolation

The withdrawal of consolation does not mean that God has withdrawn. Rather, the mode of God's presence has changed. God is now present in a more gentle and peaceful way called contemplation. "Contemplation is nothing else than a secret and peaceful and loving inflow of God" (N 1.10.6). Let us use the following image to understand the change from consolation to contemplation.

Think of the soul as an ocean where the sun dances sprightly upon its waves. This is comparable to the experience of beginners during the time of consolation in which they find delight in discursive meditation, that is, in prayer that engages the intellect and the imagination. However, one day the sky becomes overcast, and the surface of the ocean becomes dark and flat. This is comparable to beginners at the time when God withdraws consolation from them; they are unable to find delight in either meditation or the things of God. The harder they try to meditate, the worse things become; prayer becomes drier and drier. They are confused.

It is at the time they are going about their spiritual exercises with delight and satisfaction, when in their opinion the sun of divine favor is shining most brightly on them, that God darkens all this light and closes the door and the spring of sweet spiritual water they are tasting. . . . God leaves them in such darkness that they do not know which way to turn in their discursive imaginings. They cannot advance a step in meditation. . . . The change is a surprise to them because everything seems to be functioning in reverse. (N 1.8.3)

These beginners believe that God has withdrawn from them, and they frequently conclude that it is due to their lack of fervor. In consequence, they redouble their efforts to meditate but to no avail. They are thrown into confusion. Their increased effort only intensifies the dryness.

However, John gives an alternate explanation for this change. God has not withdrawn but is present to the soul in a different way. God is to be found no longer in the sprightly dance on the waves but on the bottom of the ocean, where the water is deep and still. Therefore, these beginners are looking for God in the wrong place. Since they are still seeking God in the sensual experience of consolation, they are unable to be present to God as God is present to them.

The reason for this dryness is that God transfers his goods and strength from sense to spirit. . . . If in the beginning the soul does not experience this spiritual savor and delight, but dryness and distaste, the reason is the novelty involved in this exchange. Since the palate is accustomed to these other sensory tastes, the soul still sets its eyes on them. And since, also, its spiritual palate is neither purged nor accommodated for so subtle a taste, it is unable to experience the spiritual savor and good until gradually prepared by means of this dark and obscure night. (N 1.9.4)

Since the mode of God's presence has changed, we must change our mode of prayer. We must no longer try to meditate with the intellect but rather be attentive to God's gentle presence. We must learn to sit quietly on the bottom of the ocean. "They must be content simply with a loving and peaceful attentiveness to God, and live without the concern, without the effort, and without the desire to taste or feel him. All these desires disquiet the soul and distract it from the peaceful, quiet and sweet idleness of the contemplation that is being communicated to it" (N 1.10.4).

This is what we are called to do if the mode of God's presence is being transferred to the bottom of the ocean. However, the question remains, how do we determine that this transition is taking place? To answer this question, John provides three indications or "signs."

As John begins chapter 9, he alerts us to the fact that dryness in prayer may have various causes. The cause may be due to the action of God, that is, it may be the result of God bringing a person into the dark night—"the sensory night and purgation" (N 1.9.1). However, the dryness may have a moral, emotional, or physical cause—"sin and imperfection, or weakness and lukewarmness or some bad humor or bodily indisposition" (N 1.9.1). The purpose of the three signs is to ascertain the cause of the dryness.

THE FIRST SIGN

The first [sign] is that since these souls do not get satisfaction or consolation from the things of God, they do not get any from creatures either. Since God puts a soul in this dark night in order to dry up and purge its sensory appetite, he does not allow it to find sweetness or delight in anything. Through this sign it can in all likelihood [*probablemente*] be inferred that this dryness and distaste is not the outcome of newly committed sins and imperfections. If this were so, some inclination or propensity to look for satisfaction in something other than the things of God would be felt in the sensory part, for when the appetite is allowed indulgence in some imperfection, the soul immediately feels an inclination toward it, little or great in proportion to the degree of its satisfaction and attachment. (N 1.9.2)

The beginning of this sign is a description of anhedonia. *Anhedonia* is derived from two Greek words, *an* meaning "without" and *hedone* meaning "pleasure." Anhedonia is the inability to find pleasure or satisfaction in activities that are normally pleasurable. "The first [sign] is that since these souls do not get satisfaction or consolation from the things of God, they do not get any from creatures either" (N 1.9.2).

Anhedonia may be the result of natural causes. It is a common symptom of depression, what John calls a "melancholic humor," which is frequently the result of a specific loss, such as the death of a loved one or the loss of a source of significance. In this regard, anhedonia may also be a symptom of the dark night, for beginners entering the dark night suffer specific losses. The withdrawal of consolation results in a twofold loss. It deprives beginners of pleasure, and it is a blow to their self-esteem. Anhedonia may also be the result of physical factors— "the product of some indisposition" (N 1.9.2). We all know how sickness can drain all the joy out of life.

John's point is that if the anhedonia is solely due to some physical or emotional disposition, then when the disposition has passed, our ability to find joy in the things of God will be restored. After we have determined that the lack of joy is not caused by either physical or psychological factors, we now have to inquire if a person's inability to find satisfaction in the things of God has a moral cause.

To answer this question, John focuses on the inclination of the will. If we are inclined to seek satisfaction in creatures, John says it is because we have made a choice to do so. In short, the inclination follows upon the satisfaction of the appetite. "For when the appetite is allowed indulgence in some imperfection, the soul immediately feels an inclination toward it, little or great in proportion to the degree of its satisfaction and attachment" (N 1.9.2).

However, John does not say that our inclination to seek consolation in creatures is always the result of self-indulgence, even though it is very probable—"in all likelihood [*probable-mente*]" (N 1.9.2).

It is also possible that our inclination to seek consolation in creatures is the result of the dark night. This is because in the dark night we suffer the loss of consolation. In consequence, we tend to compensate for this loss by seeking pleasure in creatures. If such is the case, we are dealing with a temporary adjustment to loss. So how can we know if our self-indulgence is a sign of spiritual regression or a temporary reaction to loss? This is where John's second sign is important.

THE SECOND SIGN

> The second sign for the discernment of this purgation is that the memory ordinarily turns to God solicitously and with painful care [*solicitud y cuidado penoso*], and the soul thinks it is not serving God but turning back, because it is aware of this distaste for the things of God. Hence it is obvious that this aversion and dryness is not the fruit of laxity and tepidity, for

lukewarm people do not care much for the things of God nor are they inwardly solicitous about them. There is, consequently, a notable difference between dryness and lukewarmness. The lukewarm are very lax and remiss in their will and spirit, and have no solicitude about serving God. Those suffering from the purgative dryness are ordinarily solicitous, concerned, and pained about not serving God. Even though the dryness may be furthered by melancholia or some other humor—as it often is—it does not thereby fail to produce its purgative effect in the appetite, for the soul will be deprived of every satisfaction and concerned only about God. If this humor is the entire cause, everything ends in displeasure and does harm to one's nature, and there are none of these desires to serve God that accompany the purgative dryness. Even though in this purgative dryness the sensory part of the soul is very cast down, slack, and feeble in its actions because of the little satisfaction it finds, the spirit is ready and strong. (N 1.9.3)

This sign gives us another example of how we can misjudge our spiritual state from an emotional perspective. There is a twofold experience contained in this sign: first, our awareness that we have a "distaste for the things of God"; and second, our reaction to our awareness. Usually, we are so focused on our awareness that we have distaste for the things of God that we erroneously conclude we're not serving God. To correct this misinterpretation, John, our third-person omniscient narrator, draws our attention to the reaction to our awareness, namely, that we are concerned that we are not serving God because of our distaste for the things of God. "The memory ordinarily turns to God solicitously and with painful care" (N 1.9.3).

These people are afraid that they have taken a wrong path. "Spiritual persons suffer considerable affliction in this night, owing not so much to the aridities they undergo as to their fear of having gone astray" (N 1.10.1). Their worry and concern that they are not serving God is an indication that the absence of consolation is not due to lukewarmness. People who are lax "have no solicitude about serving God" (N 1.9.3).

In contrast, if there is no concern about serving God, this is an indication of tepidity. "The lukewarm are very lax and remiss in their will and spirit, and have no solicitude about serving God" (N 1.9.3). In short, such people have ceased trying or at least have slackened their efforts. Such willful carelessness results in the waning of desire.

This latter part of the second sign contains a spiritual truth that goes beyond its function to help us discern if we are entering the dark night, namely, that desire is related to choice. When we change our behavior, we alter affect. The more we choose to settle into a lifestyle characterized by laxity and negligence, the more our desire to do God's will dissipates.

If we find ourselves in such a condition, we can only recover what we have lost by retracing our steps back to the right path. As St. John Climacus writes, "When the soul betrays itself, when that initial happy warmth grows cold, the reasons for such a loss ought to be carefully sought and once found, ought to be combated with all possible zeal, for the initial fervor has to turn back through that same gate through which it had slipped away."[1]

THE THIRD SIGN

The third sign for the discernment of this purgation of the senses is the powerlessness, in spite of one's efforts, to meditate and make use of the imagination, the interior sense, as was one's previous custom. At this time God does not communicate himself through the senses as he did before, by means of the discursive analysis and synthesis of ideas, but begins to communicate himself through pure spirit by an act of simple contemplation in which there is no discursive succession of thought. The exterior and interior senses of the lower part of the soul cannot attain to this contemplation. As a result the imaginative power and phantasy can no longer rest in any consideration or find support in it. (N 1.9.8)

The first part of the third sign is similar to the first sign. The inability to neither engage in discursive meditation nor derive any consolation from it is part and parcel of a person's inability to find "satisfaction or consolation from the things of God" (N 1.9.1). This inability adds to our belief that our dryness is due to our lack of fervor. In consequence, we will often redouble our efforts to meditate, which only makes us weary. "They then grow weary and strive, as was their custom, to concentrate their faculties . . . on a subject of meditation" (N 1.10.1). All this effort is not only futile but also prevents us from experiencing what God is doing within us. God is "communicat[ing] himself through pure spirit by an act of simple contemplation" (N 1.9.8).

One of the effects of the quiet, gentle presence of God (contemplation) that is beginning to be communicated in the dark night is that it produces within us "an inclination to remain alone and in quietude" (N 1.9.6). However, at the beginning of the dark night, we often do not experience this inclination. "If in the beginning the soul does not experience this spiritual savor and delight, but dryness and distaste, the reason is the novelty involved in this exchange. Since its palate is accustomed to these sensory tastes, the soul still sets its eyes on them. And since, also its spiritual palate is neither purged nor accommodated for so subtle a taste, it is unable to experience the spiritual [contemplation]" (N 1.9.4).

As a result of our inability to experience this inclination, we often continue to force ourselves to meditate discursively. In contrast, in *The Ascent of Mount Carmel*, John describes souls that are not at the beginning of the dark night. They have learned through experience that forcing themselves to meditate only increases their dryness, and when they cease their efforts to meditate, they experience their inclination to be alone in God's presence. They have discovered that they "like to remain alone in loving awareness of God, without particular considerations, in interior peace and quiet and repose" (A 2.13.5). This is why in *The Ascent of Mount Carmel* John's third sign is different from the one that he presents to us in *The Dark Night of the Soul*. "The third and surest sign is that a person likes to remain alone in loving awareness of God, without particular considerations, in interior peace and quiet and repose, and without the acts and the exercises (at least discursive, those in which one progresses from point to point) of the intellect, memory and will. Such a one prefers to remain only in a general loving awareness and knowledge of God . . . without any particular knowledge or understanding" (A 2.13.5).

CONCLUSION OF THE THREE SIGNS

John says that if we experience these three signs within ourselves, then we can safely conclude that God is gently drawing us into the dark night, in which the mode of the divine presence is becoming more and more a general loving awareness of God.

The three signs may be summarized as a threefold experience. I can't meditate. I don't want to meditate. All I want to do is to rest gently in an awareness of God's presence.

A NEW ATTACHMENT

The capacity to experience the general loving awareness of God is an acquired taste. John compares it to the Israelites who, after being weaned away from the savory fleshpots of Egypt (consolation), developed a palate to taste "the delicate sweetness of the angelic manna" (contemplation; N 1.9.5).

Unfortunately, this growth poses a danger; a new attachment can be formed. When God draws us away from the pleasures of this world by means of consolation, we can become attached to consolation. Likewise, when God withdraws consolation, we can become attached to the delicate peace of contemplation. In short, we can transfer our attachment from one pleasure to another. As John says, regarding a person who is beginning to experience the peace of contemplation, "the soul desires or tries to experience it" (N 1.9.6).

The desire and effort to experience the peace that contemplation imparts is counterproductive because the delicacy of contemplation is of such a nature that it eludes the grasp of the will. "It is like air that escapes when one tries to grasp it in one's hand" (N 1.9.6). What we need to do is to develop a nongrasping, nonpossessive attitude. "The attitude necessary in this night of sense is to pay no attention to discursive meditation since this is not the time for it. All that is required is freedom of soul. They must be content simply with a loving and peaceful attentiveness to God, and live without the concern, without the effort, and without the desire to taste or feel him. All these desires disquiet the soul and distract it from the peaceful quiet, and sweet idleness of the contemplation that is being communicated to it" (N 1.10.4).

This new attitude pertains to the spiritual life in general and contemplative prayer in particular. Regarding the spiritual life, when we are being led into the dark night, we should "live without the concern, without the effort, and without the desire to taste or feel him" (N 1.10.4). In short, we should stop worrying, stop trying, and stop desiring to experience God. We are called to be detached from seeking to experience God, in the form of either consolation or contemplation. Regarding contemplative prayer in particular, John says that we must be like a model for a painting. We must learn to "sit still" and cease fidgeting with the faculties of the intellect and imagination.

When we are in the initial part of the transition from discursive meditation to contemplation, we may find ourselves vacillating between two worlds. Even though we have a desire to rest in a loving and peaceful awareness of God's presence, our desire to meditate can still cling to us. "Similarly, any operation, affection, or thought a soul might cling to when it wants to abide in interior peace and idleness would cause distraction and disquietude" (N 1.10.5).

Not only does clinging to a desire to meditate deprive us of what we want, it also hinders the work of God. "If a model for the painting . . . should move because of a desire to do something, the artist would be unable to finish and the work would be spoiled" (N 1.10.5). The work that the Divine Artist is accomplishing in us by means of contemplation is "the enkindling and burning of love . . . for contemplation is nothing else than a secret and peaceful and loving inflow of God" (N 1.10.6).

For Reflection

When you are praying, have you ever felt that God is drawing you into the silence of your heart? Have you ever been "conscious . . . of being placed in silence" (F 3.35)?

When this happens, are you able to "be content simply with a loving and peaceful attentiveness to God, and live without the concern, without the effort, and without the desire to taste or feel him" (N 1.10.4)?

NIGHT 1.11

The Fire of Love

❧

There are two possible reasons this enkindling "of love is not commonly felt at the outset" (N 1.11.1): "either because it does not have a chance to take hold, owing to the impurity of the sensory part," or "because the soul for want of understanding has not made within itself a peaceful place for it" (N 1.11.1). Let us consider each reason in turn.

IMAGINING AND DOING

A few years ago, during my annual physical, tests showed that my blood pressure, cholesterol, and blood sugar levels were elevated. As I sat on the examination table, trying my best to suck in my potbelly, my doctor said to me, "If you want to stay off medication, you have to change your lifestyle; you have to diet and exercise."

When I left the office, I was armed with resolve. I imagined how easy it would be to moderate my intake of food, eat healthy meals, and incorporate an exercise program into my daily schedule. However, imagining and doing are two completely different realities. In this regard, reflecting upon the difference between contemplating his conversion and embracing it, St. Augustine writes, "It is one thing to see, from a wooded mountain top, the land of peace . . . and it is quite another thing to keep to the way which leads there."[1]

At this juncture in his life, Augustine was unable to take hold of the "peaceful and loving inflow of God" (N 1.10.6) that was being imparted to him because he was impeded by "the lion and the dragon" that "lurk[ed] in ambush" upon his path. In other words, as he ventured upon a new way of life, the inveterate habits of his old life reared their ugly heads. The grace of spiritual conversion is not magic; it does not automatically undo the ingrained habits of a lifetime.

Such is the reality when we begin to receive the grace of contemplation. Although "a certain longing for God" is engendered in us by contemplation, it "does not have a chance to take hold [of us], owing to the impurity of the sensory part [of our souls]" (N 1.11.1). In consequence, we do not find "within [ourselves] a peaceful place for [contemplation]" (N 1.11.1). This is because our "imperfect affections and habits" that have been acquired over a lifetime result in "a distracted and inattentive spirit" (N 2.2.2).

We can all relate to this experience. As we sit down and attempt to rest in that peaceful place that contemplation has created within us, our minds are drawn into a swirl of emotionally laden thoughts and images. Our distracted and inattentive spirit does not give contemplation a chance to take hold of us. Yes, there are times when we can rest quietly in God, but often this is not the case. So what should we do? The first thing we need to do is look at distractions from a spiritual perspective rather than from an emotional perspective.

From time to time, a person in spiritual direction will ask, "How can I rid myself of distractions in prayer?" My response is, "Why would you want to do that?" The person usually looks at me with a puzzled expression, as if to say, "Well, isn't the answer self-evident? So I can pray better."

No, the answer is not self-evident. Sometimes our primary motive for not wanting distractions in prayer is more sensual than spiritual, namely, we want to feel peaceful. This is an example of how we often interpret the spiritual from an emotional perspective. So what should we do when we are beginning to experience contemplation and are assailed by distractions?

First, try to be at peace. Know that distractions are a normal manifestation of our spiritual condition. John tells us that when we enter the night of the spirit, even after we have been purified in the night of sense, we still retain "the natural dullness everyone contracts through sin, and a distracted and inattentive spirit" (N 2.2.2).

Second, having accepted this fact, approach distractions from a spiritual perspective instead of from an emotional one. Our focus should be on not what we feel in prayer but what we do. Let's say that during a half hour of prayer your mind wanders one hundred times, and one hundred times you choose to recenter it upon God. You might feel that your distractions have created a barrier between God and yourself. However, John's evaluation of your prayer would be much different than yours. He might say something to you like this: "I know that you feel discouraged because of your distractions, but you need to realize that your prayer is very transformative. Yes, you had one hundred distractions, but you fail to recognize that you also made one hundred acts of the will, which are one hundred acts of love. Remember that the goal of the spiritual life is uniting your *will* to God in love."[2]

FOR A WANT OF UNDERSTANDING

Over the years I have worked with people in spiritual direction who feel guilty because they find it increasingly more difficult to pray the rosary.

Directee: I begin saying the rosary, but halfway through, it becomes so labored that I have to force myself to continue, so much so that sometimes I just give up trying.

Director: When this happens, what do you *want* to do?

Directee: Nothing. I just want to sit quietly.

Director: And what do you feel as you are sitting quietly?

Directee: Often I feel the peace of God's presence, but then I feel guilty because I think that I'm being lazy. If I really loved our Blessed Mother, I should try harder to say the rosary.

Director: Have you ever considered that your desire to sit quietly in God's presence as you are saying the rosary is leading you into contemplative prayer? And have you ever thought that when this happens, and you choose to stop saying the rosary and sit quietly in God's presence, that you are helping to fulfill Mary's maternal role in salvation?

Directee: I don't know what you mean.

Director: In many icons, Mary is holding the child Jesus and her right hand is pointing to him. This is symbolic of Mary's role in salvation, to lead us to Jesus. Has it ever occurred to you that when you are praying the rosary and you want to sit in God's presence, it is because Mary has accomplished her task? She has led you to Jesus.

I have found this explanation helpful to people whom God is leading into contemplative prayer but who "for want of understanding [have not made within themselves] a peaceful place for [contemplation]" (N 1.11.1). They often do not understand that the knowledge that they were "gradually acquiring through the labor of meditation on particular ideas has . . . been converted into habitual and substantial, general loving knowledge" (A 2.14.2). Once God has accomplished this task, a person who tries to return to meditation is "like someone who turns from what has already been done in order to do it again, or like one who leaves a city only to re-enter it" (N 1.10.1).

In *A Doorway to Silence: The Contemplative Use of the Rosary*, Robert Llewelyn gives the following image regarding the relationship between vocal and contemplative prayer:

> You will be helped if you hold this picture in mind for all repetitive prayer. The words are like the banks of a river and the prayer is like the river itself. The banks are necessary to give direction and to keep the river deep and flowing. But it is the river with which we are concerned. So in prayer it is the inclination of the heart to God which alone matters. The words are there to assist and support this fundamental need. They are the framework in which the prayer is held. The words are not the prayer. The prayer lies always beyond the words. As the river moves into the sea, the banks drop away. So, too, as we move into the deeper sense of God's presence the words fall away and . . . we shall be left in silence in the ocean of God's love.[3]

In contemplative prayer, "the soul becomes aware of being attracted by the love of God . . . without knowing how or where this attraction originates" (N 1.11.1). This attraction has its origin in the ocean of God's presence. It draws us into silence beyond words, though the doorway into the silence is often words. As John writes, "Seek in reading and you will find in meditation; knock in prayer and it will be opened to you in contemplation" (SLL 158). To enter into the quiet presence of God, we are bid to "knock" gently, with a word or a phrase that quiets the mind and disposes the heart to be drawn by God into silence.

THE ENKINDLING OF LOVE

Although the fire of love is not "commonly felt" (N 1.11.1) at the outset of the dark night, due to the soul's impurity and lack of understanding, "the enkindling of love" is "experienced from time to time" (N 1.11.1). However, more often than not, what is experienced at this time are "longings for God" or "a living thirst" for God (N 1.11.1). This thirst is "living" because it is an experience of God. Our longing is both a hunger for God and an experience of God for whom we hunger. Thus, our deepest desire is both human and divine.

The dark night enkindles in us a yearning to leave behind our earthly desires and be united to the abundant riches of God. However, an invitation is not a response; to be beckoned forth is not to go forth. We must choose what we will do. The desire that is enkindled is the work of God; it is the passive aspect of the dark night. The active part of the dark night is our response.

In *The Spiritual Canticle*, John distinguishes the passive from the active aspects of the dark night. The passive aspect is our desire for God, which is enkindled by God. The active aspect is our response to our desire—seeking God. Because the bride (soul) is wounded with desire by her Bridegroom (God), she "longs for union with him" (C 1.2). In order to fulfill this longing, she decides "to go out searching for him . . . to seek him through works" (C 3.2). "She must practice the virtues and engage in the spiritual exercises of both the active and the contemplative life" (C 3.1).

Since in *The Dark Night of the Soul*, John's primary focus is on the passive aspect of transformation, it is important to remember that the passive aspect of the dark night (what God does) cannot be separated from its active dimension (our response). To do so is to risk misunderstanding John's teaching. For example, in the next two chapters, John enumerates the various benefits of the arid night of sense. Unless we realize that these benefits are inseparable from our cooperation, it is easy to derive the erroneous impression that they occur simply as a result of experiencing the inflow of "this dry contemplation" (N 1.13.10).

For Reflection

"O God, you are my God, I seek you, my soul thirsts for you . . . as in a dry and weary land where there is no water for whom I long . . . so I looked for you in the sanctuary" (Ps 63:1–2).

When your "longings for God" become "a living thirst" (N 1.11.1), you need not look for God because your thirst for God *is* an experience of the God for whom you long.

Have you ever considered that your thirst for God is an indication that God has found you?

NIGHT 1.12

The Benefits of Self-Knowledge

$\sim\!\sim\!\sim$

At the beginning of *The Dark Night*, John used *being nursed* as a metaphor of God caressing us with consolation (N 1.1.2). Now, he uses *being weaned* as an image of God withdrawing consolation (N 1.12.1). Though we experience this weaning as a loss, John tells us that it is a gain. From an emotional perspective, we may feel we are regressing; however, from a spiritual perspective, we are progressing. Using the event of Isaac's "weaning" (*quitó*) as an image of entering the passive night of sense, John allows us to see what is happening from God's perspective. Though Isaac (the soul) is mourning the loss of his mother's milk, Abraham (God) is rejoicing over his son's growth. "God has now taken from this soul its swaddling clothes, he has put it down from his arms and is making it walk alone" (N 1.12.1).

The word that John uses for weaning, *quitó*, accurately describes the experience of being deprived of consolation. It means to take away, to withdraw, to deprive, and even to be robbed. Being suddenly deprived of "delicate and sweet food" and made to "eat bread with crust" (N 1.12.1) is both a jarring and sobering experience. Without the experience of consolation, we are not only deprived of the sweetness of God's presence but also no longer able to maintain the illusion of our self-importance. In short, our smug self-satisfaction and complacency is shattered. However, as painful as this self-knowledge is, it is a necessary condition for a true relationship with God to be established. "[The soul] considers itself to be nothing and finds no satisfaction in self because it is aware that of itself it neither does nor can do anything" (N 1.12.2). *Of itself* it can do nothing. This is the first bitter morsel of self-knowledge that we must swallow—to accept that self-sufficiency is an illusion. We are faced with our powerlessness; we cannot do anything by ourselves.

During the time of consolation, we were dressed in "festive garments," but when consolation was withdrawn, we donned the "garments of labor, dryness and desolation" (N 1.12.2). No longer is prayer a joy; no longer is the practice of virtue effortless. Prayer is now dry and virtue laborious. Stripped of our spiritual persona, we stand naked before our insignificance and powerlessness. Yet, John tells us that this self-knowledge is "the first and chief benefit of this dry and dark night of contemplation" (N 1.12.2).

There is a threefold benefit derived from this self-knowledge. The first we have already mentioned; we have been humbled and brought into a realistic relationship with ourselves. In turn, the humility that has been acquired through self-knowledge changes our relationships to both God and neighbor.

OUR RELATIONSHIP TO SELF AND GOD

When I was a cocky adolescent, one night after supper, I said to my mother, "Hey, Vera, that was a good meal." My mother looked me straight in the eye and said in a slow, deliberate tone of voice, "Excuse me, young man, *what* did you call me?" I froze. I knew that I had overstepped my bounds by calling my mother by her first name. I addressed her as my equal and was promptly put in my place.

The pride that consolation gives rise to in beginners tends to turn them into cocky adolescents in relationship to God. John says "that the satisfying delight [of consolation] made them more daring (*atrevido*) with God than [is] proper" (N 1.12.3). *Atrevido* can also be translated as bold, forward, confident, or free. Beginners in their unweaned boldness are too forward with God; they presume a familiarity with God that is neither proper nor fitting.

Beginners are also like spoiled children. They feel entitled to do what they want to do in order to procure consolation. Because they have a "lack of the loving fear and respect they owe to God's grandeur, they do not hesitate to insist boldly that their confessors allow them the frequent reception of Communion" (N 1.6.4).

However, when they are brought into the dark night of sense, their insistence is impotent. They are not in control; God is not at their beck and call. God will decide when consolation is given and when it will be withheld. In consequence, they begin to "commune with God more respectfully (*comedimiento*) and courteously (*cortesania*)" (N 1.12.3).

In addition to politeness and courtesy, the Spanish words *comedimiento* and *cortesania* contain elements of deference and obsequiousness. John's culture was deeply conscious of social rank, which was reflected in language. A sixteenth-century Spaniard would never address a lord with the familiar *tú* but always with the formal and respectful *vos* (vous) or *usted*.

If we speak a different language, says philosopher Ludwig Wittgenstein, we begin to perceive a different world. Such is the case when we begin to commune humbly and respectfully with God. By discarding our arrogant familiarity with God, we become disposed to enter into true intimacy with God. Humility and the experience of our wretchedness is the low doorway through which we must stoop in order to enter into the vast spaciousness of God's grandeur. "God will give illumination by bestowing on the soul not only knowledge of its own misery and lowliness but also knowledge of his grandeur and majesty" (N 1.12.4). In short, self-knowledge and knowledge of God are inseparably linked, the former being the wellspring of the latter. "We conclude that self-knowledge flows first from this dry night, and that from this knowledge as from its source proceeds the other knowledge of God" (N 1.12.5).

Thus, we cannot know God unless we know ourselves. Being conscious of our misery is not only a prelude to our knowledge of God; it is a necessary condition. As John writes, quoting St. Augustine, *"Let me know myself, Lord, and I will know you.* For as the philosophers say, one extreme is clearly known by the other" (N 1.12.5).

The reverse of St. Augustine's prayer is also true. As St. Teresa writes, "We shall never completely know ourselves if we don't strive to know God. By gazing at His grandeur, we get in touch with our own lowliness; by looking at His purity, we shall see our own filth. . . . Something white seems much whiter when next to something black, and vice versa with the black next to the white" (IC 1.2.9–10).

Even though John's teaching in this chapter regarding the relationship between self-knowledge and knowledge of God primarily follows St. Augustine's sequence that knowledge of God follows upon knowledge of self, John also refers to St. Teresa's perspective that we can come to know ourselves through our knowledge of God. In this regard, John references the book of Job, where Job is humbled as the result of being overwhelmed by an experience of God's grandeur (N 1.12.3).

Therefore, whether self-knowledge follows upon an experience of God or vice versa is not the issue. The core of John's teaching is that true self-knowledge is inseparable from knowledge of God.

OUR RELATIONSHIP TO OUR NEIGHBOR: FROM JUDGING TO ESTEEMING

The self-knowledge that we acquire in the dark night transforms our relationship to our neighbor. During the time of consolation, our pride "condemn[ed] others . . . and gave expression to this criticism like the pharisee who despised the publican while he boasted and praised God for the good deeds he himself accomplished" (N 1.2.1). Now, the humility that flows from self-knowledge has changed everything; the pharisee has been transformed into the publican. "Through this humility acquired by means of self-knowledge . . . the thought of their being more advanced than others does not even occur [to them]. From this humility stems love of neighbor, for they esteem them and do not judge them as they did before when they were aware that they enjoyed an intense fervor while others did not. These persons know only their misery and keep it so much in sight that they have no opportunity to watch anyone else's conduct . . . [and] also became silent concerning his neighbor" (N 1.12.7–8).

When beginners are swimming in consolation, they tend to judge their neighbor rashly because they do "not seem to have the kind of devotion" (N 1.2.1) that the beginners themselves possess. However, as consolation is withdrawn, they are in a position to learn two important spiritual truths. First, during the time of consolation, they often misjudge their spiritual condition and think that their will to practice virtue is strong, when in fact it's quite fragile. Their pride creates the illusion that their spiritual edifice is stable. In reality it is wobbly. Once the emotional support of consolation is withdrawn, it collapses like a house of cards. And if these beginners are very proud, God may let them sin seriously—though actually this is an act of his mercy. As St. Thomas Aquinas teaches, "In order to overcome their pride, God punishes certain men by allowing them to fall into sins of the flesh, which though they be less grievous are more evidently shameful. . . . From this the gravity of pride is made manifest. For just as a wise physician, in order to cure a worse disease, allows the patient to contract one that is less dangerous, so the sin of pride is shown to be more grievous by the very fact that, as a remedy, God allows men to fall into other sins" ST II, II, q. 162, a. 6).

In addition, St. Thérèse believed that God sometimes allows us to fall into sin, not only to humble our pride, but also to allow us to "experience in ourselves the same weaknesses which we deplore in others . . . [and] see ourselves fallen into those faults, we are then more prompt to excuse them in others."[1] In short, as we experience our moral and spiritual weakness, we are less apt to judge harshly the weaknesses of others. This is the second important spiritual truth that beginners learn as consolation is withdrawn. If this truth becomes an abiding part of our consciousness, it will arguably be the most important aspect of our spiritual life, for it will simultaneously keep us humble before God and forgiving and compassionate toward our neighbor.

For Reflection

[Abba Moses said,] "If the monk does not think in his heart that he is a sinner, God will not hear him." The brother said, "What does that mean, to think in his heart that he is a sinner?" Then the old man said, "When someone is occupied with his own faults, he does not see those of his neighbour."[2]

This is fruit of self-knowledge. When grace focuses our minds on our sinfulness, we are not preoccupied with the faults of others. As a result of this "self-knowledge," we "do not judge as [we] did before. . . . [We] know only [our] misery and keep it so much in sight that [we] have no opportunity to watch anyone else's conduct" (N 1.12.7–8). Being aware of our own sinfulness is painful. However, it is an antidote to rash judging, what St. Francis de Sales calls "spiritual jaundice [that] causes all things to appear evil to the eyes of those infected by it."[3]

Have you ever experienced a reduction or cessation of judging your neighbor as a consequence of growing in self-knowledge of your own sinfulness?

Other Benefits of the Night of Sense

EXCESS AND DEFECT

When beginners are bathed in consolation, they inordinately "crave . . . spiritual exercises" (N 1.13.1). Conversely, when they enter the "arid and obscure night" of sense, they often fail to perform their spiritual exercises. Consequently, they "fail through defect rather than excess" (N 1.13.1). Because they find their spiritual exercises to be "distasteful and laborious" (N 1.13.1), they often discontinue them. They fail through excess when they receive consolation, and they fail through defect when consolation is withdrawn.

EAGERNESS TO CONCLUDE

"I am eager to conclude this dark night [of sense] in order to pass on to the important doctrine we have concerning the other night [of spirit]" (N 1.13.3). John's eagerness is manifested in his cursory treatment of the other capital sins. This is in marked contrast to his detailed treatment of pride in the previous chapter. Here are two examples. Regarding spiritual lust, John writes, "The soul is freed of those impurities we noted" (N 1.13.2). Regarding spiritual gluttony, John writes,

"Let it suffice to say that the soul is liberated from all the imperfections we mentioned" (N 1.13.3).

In spite of John's eagerness to conclude his treatment of the dark night of sense, we should not pass over this chapter too quickly because it contains a benefit of the dark night that is important for us to understand. It is a psycho-spiritual dynamic of the passive night of the spirit that we will consider in greater depth in book two of *The Dark Night*. The benefit is paradoxical. "The soul dwells in spiritual peace and tranquility" (N 1.13.3) and "bears a habitual remembrance of God" (N 1.13.4) while it experiences "aridities and darknesses" (N 1.12.1). The key to understanding the paradox is contained in John's phrase "dry contemplation" (N 1.13.10).

As contemplation deprives the sensual part of our nature of consolation, it simultaneously strengthens and nourishes the spiritual part. Understanding that we can experience God present in our spirit, while we feel that God is absent in our senses, is crucial for our comprehension of the psycho-spiritual dynamics of what follows. For there, we will encounter a similar dynamic. "In the midst of these dark and loving afflictions, the soul feels a certain companionship and an interior strength" (N 2.11.7). In short, in the midst of feeling alone we experience a presence that sustains us.

For Reflection

In the fervor of consolation, beginners frequently practice many nonobligatory private devotions, which become burdensome when consolation is withdrawn.

CONTINUED

They cannot give up these practices because of a false sense of obligation. Since consolation was often fused with the recitation of certain devotional prayers, some people feel it would be ungrateful to discontinue these prayers, even when God is leading them into contemplative prayer. In the fervor of consolation, it is not difficult to imagine some beginners saying, "I promise you, God, I will recite these prayers every day for the rest of my life." Then, they feel an obligation to do so and bind themselves to "vows" made in fervor.

Have you ever felt obligated to continue to pray some devotion after it has served its purpose?

The Trials of the Committed Soul

What happens when we have endured the confusion and dryness of the initial transition from the state of beginners to the state of proficients? What happens to us when we have been freed from the restrictions of discursive meditation and weaned from the sweetness of consolation and are beginning to receive the inflow of God called contemplation, which "teaches [us] secretly and instructs [us] in the perfection of love" (N 1.5.1)? That all depends upon our dedication. Are we generous or niggardly in our response to God? As St. Thérèse expresses it, "I understood [that] there were many degrees of perfection and each soul was free to respond to the advances of Our Lord, to do little or much for Him, in a word, to *choose* among the sacrifices He was asking" (S 27).

In this chapter, John lists three trials that individuals whom God is calling to a deeper process of transformation must be willing to suffer: intense sexual temptations, anger toward God (temptations to blaspheme), and mental confusion regarding coming to peace with discerning God's will (scrupulosity). Though these trials should not be considered an exhaustive list, they are paradigmatic of what a person may suffer in the dark night of the spirit. Let us consider each in turn.[1]

THE SPIRIT OF FORNICATION

> For those who must afterward enter into the other more oppressive night of the spirit in order to reach the divine union of love—because not everyone but only a few usually reach this union—this night [the sensory night] is ordinarily accompanied by burdensome trials and sensory temptations that last a long time, and with some longer than with others. An angel of Satan [2 Cor 12:7], which is the spirit of fornication, is given to some to buffet their senses with strong abominable temptations, and afflict their spirit with foul thoughts and very vivid images, which sometimes is a pain worse than death for them. (N 1.14.1)

In order to understand both the psychological and spiritual reasons for these temptations of lust, we need to locate them where they emerge on the spiritual path. John deals with them in the last chapter of book one of *The Dark Night*, which is a transition chapter that bridges his treatment of the night of sense and the night of the spirit. In other words, he is writing of persons who have been on the spiritual path for many years and who "have a more considerable capacity and strength for suffering" in contrast to persons who "are never wholly in the night or wholly out of it" (N 1.14.5). Thus, John is indicating that these temptations are often more intense in people who have fully entered into the dark night and are open to being led by God into a deeper process of transformation. To answer why these people are often bombarded with intense sexual temptations is not an easy task, for such temptations may be the result of any number of different causes or combination of causes. Let us explore three possibilities: seeking relief, assuaging anxiety, and the emergence of regressive longings.

Seeking Relief

When we accept God's invitation to enter the dark night of sense in earnest, we choose a lifestyle that bridles the pleasure principle by mortifying our inordinate appetites. Human nature naturally rebels against such restrictions and presents its cravings to the conscious mind in the form of images. Perhaps the most basic reason the sexual images are "foul" (in Spanish, *feas*, which can carry with it connotations of brutality and moral depravity) has to do with the brute strength of pent-up sexual tension that seeks relief.

Assuaging Anxiety

"He started thinking about women again. He let pictures rise in the dark, all kinds; clothed, naked, asleep, awake, drinking, dancing. . . . A little spark of desire began to glow. . . . He blew on it deliberately. Nothing like lust for keeping fear at a distance."[2] This observation by C. S. Lewis regarding the relationship between lust and fear is relevant to our topic because there is much anxiety in the dark night.

One source of anxiety that is native to the dark night is the result of relinquishing control over one's life and allowing oneself to be led by God down dark and unfamiliar paths. "As regards this road to union, entering on the road means leaving one's own road" and passing "beyond the interior and exterior limits of [one's] own nature" (A 2.4.5).

Who has not known the cold fear and trembling anxiety that ensues from being confronted by God's call to venture into an untried territory of life? Such experiences can trigger our deepest insecurities and inadequacies and make us feel defective and unfit for life. They resurrect our self-doubts that feed our deepest suspicions that we are nothing but frightened children masquerading as adults. The psyche instinctively attempts to anesthetize this devouring anxiety by calling to mind sexual images (among other types of images) that are equally as savage as the anxiety that it tries to assuage. Therefore, we shouldn't be shocked or frightened at the foulness, the rawness, the pure animality, or even the perversity of the images that come to our minds during times of severe anxiety. The intensity of the sexual passion that is evoked by the image is an attempt on the part of the psyche to override the feeling of fragmentation and restore psychic equilibrium.

We also need to keep in mind that the spiritual life is not a cubicle isolated from the rest of life; it is God's grace operating in us as we are. If, for example, we have a history of emotional abandonment, we have probably learned to numb our high degree of separation anxiety by some means, whether food, alcohol, drugs, work, or sex. Therefore, it should not be surprising that when we are being led by God to journey deeper into the thicket of transformation, beyond the rim of the familiar into the hinterland of the unknown, old and deeply ingrained patterns of self-soothing will reassert themselves with a vengeance. John says as much in stanza 3 of *The Spiritual Canticle* where the Bride, as she begins to seek her Beloved by practicing the virtues and entering into a deeper process of detachment, encounters "wild beasts" that attempt to block her path. One of these beasts is "the natural rebellions of the flesh . . . that sets itself up as though on the frontier to oppose the spiritual journey" (C 3.10).

We cannot bypass our human nature in the dark night because it "brings to light" (N 2.5.1) all that is within us that needs to be healed and redeemed, for the "dark night is an inflow of God into the soul which purges it of its habitual ignorances and imperfections, natural and spiritual" (N 2.5.1), which "the soul has contracted throughout its life" (N 2.6.5). In psychological terms, there is a lifting of repression; things that have been pushed down into the unconscious begin to surface in order to be transformed.[3]

The Emergence of Regressive Longings

Lust or any form of sensuality can be compensatory. It offers the committed person relief from the monotony that accompanies steadfast fidelity to the nitty-gritty of daily life and attempts to compensate for the many losses that one incurs as the result of choosing to do God's will. Let's take an example.

Ann is married and has two children ages two and four. Last year she made a difficult decision to curtail her work as an English instructor at a nearby state university in order to spend more time at home with her children. Although Ann believes she has made the right decision, she misses teaching and the intellectual stimulation of her colleagues. Also, the monotony of being a full-time mom is beginning to take its toll.

Recently, she has found herself daydreaming about an old boyfriend named Bob with whom she used to go steady in college. At first, these daydreams were intermittent, but recently Bob has been on her mind constantly, and sometimes Ann feels he is with her. Bob's "presence" produces a bittersweet mood in Ann that is so poignant at times that it makes her cry. At other times, his image creates a strange melancholic mood within her, a nostalgia for something she cannot name, a kind of paradise lost yearning for something she cannot fully grasp.

Ann feels guilty because she believes she is being unfaithful to her husband. She is also confused. She doesn't understand what is happening to her. She is too ashamed to talk to anyone about her romantic/sexual feelings toward a man she hasn't seen for nearly twenty years, and she is beginning to wonder if she is doing something wrong. "Maybe if I prayed more or was more attentive to doing God's will, these fantasies and feelings would not be plaguing me." But Ann has been very faithful to her spiritual life and has taken the following of God's will very seriously. Paradoxically, Ann's faithfulness may be the catalyst that is triggering her "very vivid images" (N 1.14.1) of Bob.

Ann's choice to curtail her career and spend more time with her children has exacted sacrifices from her, the depth of which she is not fully conscious. Even though Ann is still teaching on a limited basis, she is unconsciously mourning her lifelong dream of becoming a full professor with a brilliant academic career. The mourning of her dream, coupled with the loss of intellectual stimulation and the burden of a thousand and one thankless tasks of being a mom, is wearing on Ann. It is within this context that we can begin to understand Ann's daydreams about Bob.

To comprehend the reasons Ann is having these fantasies, we must not focus too narrowly on her romantic/sexual feelings toward Bob but rather interpret them within the emotional atmosphere that surrounds her memories of Bob. The early twentieth-century French novelist Marcel Proust once compared the recesses of memory to thousands of vases that are situated on the various layers of our past and are filled with atmospheres reminiscent of particular periods of our lives. Using this image, we can view the atmosphere or emotional tonality that permeates Ann's memory of Bob as everything that was going on in her life during her college days: in short, who she was, her philosophy of life, her dreams for her future, and so forth.

Ann's college days were charged with excitement. Living in a college dorm away from home for the first time in her life, with the freedom to experiment with drugs and sex, made her feel alive. In addition, Ann was free of the worries of adult responsibilities of being a breadwinner, wife, and mother, and she dreamed of becoming an English professor. Bob was an integral part of Ann's dream. They talked about marriage and fantasized about their future life together. Both were academically orientated and aspired to careers in teaching English.

Considering the compensatory nature of the psyche, we can understand why it would choose this period in Ann's life as a means to try to offset the losses of her present situation. However, we must continue to dig deeper to completely understand the strength of Ann's "very vivid images." Because our psychic life is an organic unity (or one *suppositum* as John would put it), the longings and dreams of Ann's college days are rooted in all the unconscious desires, the unmourned dreams of her childhood and the deep regressive "longings for mother, the nostalgia for the source from which we came."[4]

When the tasks or challenges of life become too heavy for us to bear, the deep regressive longings of our psyche come to the surface. All we want is to return to the womb, to a place of complete security and peace; we want to be free of all worries, concerns, and responsibilities, and to be relieved of the anguish of conscience and choice. We yearn for absolute freedom to do whatever we want and simply to be left alone.

Our regressive longings beckon us to flee life by numbing ourselves with food, drink, drugs, sex, sleep, and so on; by hurling ourselves headlong into various forms of frantic activity; or by escaping into fantasy. All these forms of escape attempt to compensate for the monotony of life. Ann's fantasies about Bob fall into this category; they present to her an idealized life that is in stark contrast to her present situation. So how should we assess Ann's fantasies?

From a psychological perspective, we can view Ann's fantasies as a natural phenomenon of the psyche. They are the psyche's attempt to soothe pain; they are expressive of the pleasure principle that is embedded in our nature. However, from a spiritual perspective, Ann's fantasies are part of the cross that follows upon her choice to do God's will. Her choice to endure her fantasies as she chooses to remain faithful to God's will is an example of what John calls the "passive night." The passive purification that Ann must endure consists in not giving into her regressive longings.

We find an archetypical image of this purification in Odysseus's encounter with the Sirens. The Sirens are nymphs who live on an island and lure unsuspecting sailors to a watery grave. They do so by singing sweetly of a sailor's past. Their song evokes such an irresistible longing in the sailor that it makes him abandon his journey and swim toward the island.

As Odysseus sails by the island of the Sirens on his way home to Ithaca, he protects his men from hearing the Sirens' enchanting voices by filling their ears with wax, while he, with ears unplugged, has his men bind him to the mast of the ship. This image of Odysseus enduring the Sirens' song as his men faithfully ply their oars and row toward home is a symbol of an important aspect of the transformation of the passive night. Transformation occurs when we remain steadfast in doing God's will while enduring all the enticing allurements that wage war against us.

Like the fish that jumped out of the river and attempted to swallow Tobias, the regressive longings and inordinate appetites that threaten to devour us, once wrestled with, become food and medicine for the journey (see Tobit 6). As Jean-Pierre de Caussade comments on this scriptural passage, "The very monsters in [Tobias's] path give him nourishment and remedies; the one that attacks him in order to devour him becomes his food."[5] Or as John puts it, our imperfections and inordinate appetites are the "fuel" of transformation (N 2.10.5). Ann's fantasies can be understood within this context. They are deep tendencies of her soul that need to come to the surface and be endured in order to be transformed.

A BLASPHEMOUS SPIRIT

> At other times a blasphemous spirit is added; it commingles intolerable blasphemies with all one's thoughts and ideas. Sometimes these blasphemies are so strongly suggested to the imagination that the soul is almost made to pronounce them, which is a grave torment to it. (N 1.14.2)

What does John mean by a blasphemous spirit? To answer this question, we must recall the type of person that John is writing about and where he or she is situated on the spiritual path. He is referring to individuals who have said yes to God and are standing on a threshold of being asked to say yes again, on a deeper level. The "blasphemous spirit" is our resistance to change.

This resistance is an aspect of the unconverted part of ourselves that the divine fire of contemplation brings to consciousness in order that it might be transformed (N 2.10.1). It is part of the "natural and vicious darknesses" (F 1.22) that arise out of our innermost depths that need to be expelled. "This divine purge stirs up all the foul and vicious humors of which the soul was never before aware" (N 2.10.2).

"When this flame shines on the soul, since its light is excessively brilliant, it shines within the darknesses of the soul, which are also excessive. Persons then feel their natural and vicious darknesses that are contrary to the supernatural light" (F 1.22). Our natural darkness becomes "vicious" when God's light shines upon our innermost depths. We react like a fearful animal that has been cornered; it feels threatened and trapped and fights for its life. The people that John is writing about in this chapter feel trapped. In consequence of their spiritual growth, they find it increasing more painful to say no to God. Since God has become more and more the center of their lives, they experience a refusal to do God's will as a deep act of self-betrayal. Simply put, when they say no to God, they find it more difficult to live with themselves. They deeply know the truth of John's admonition: "Since a double measure of bitterness must follow the doing of your own will, do not do it even through you remain in single bitterness" (SLL 17).

As God beckons these people to a deeper conversion of heart, they feel trapped; their inner resistance balks at saying yes, but they cannot live with themselves if they say no. They are torn between biddings and its forbiddings. Jungian analyst Marie-Louise von Franz captures from a psychological perspective this conflict that arises when God breaks into our lives.

> The ego . . . is wounded because something greater [the self] breaks into its life. Which is why Dr. Jung says that it means tremendous suffering to get in touch with the process of individuation. It causes a tremendous wound because, put simply, we are robbed of the capacity for arranging our own lives according to our own wishes. . . . To be deprived of an evening out, or a trip, is not so bad, but there are more serious matters where we greatly want something which is suddenly vetoed by the unconscious. We feel broken and crucified, caught in a trap or imprisoned,

nailed against the cross. With your whole heart and mind you want to do something, and the unconscious vetoes it.[6]

The blasphemous spirit that is engendered by feeling trapped and being robbed of the capacity to arrange one's life according to one's wishes is fanned into resentment when we feel that those around us are not in the same situation. Céline, the sister of St. Thérèse, once felt that God was asking her "to renounce some legitimate pleasures which other sisters could enjoy in peace."[7] Her resentment was due to the fact not that God was asking her to renounce some legitimate pleasures but that God wasn't asking others to do so. This is an important fact to keep in mind in our consideration of the temptation to blaspheme God, because often the temptation is not directed toward God but displaced upon people in our environment. Let us consider the following example.

In your workplace or community there's a "problem person" whose behavior is disturbing everyone. People are tiptoeing around the situation. However, after prayer and counsel, you've come to the conclusion that God is asking you to confront this individual. You are furious with others for what you have labeled as their obtuseness, apathy, and lack of nerve; yet, you are also envious of them. You wish that you were not burdened with a heightened sense of consciousness.

As we journey deeper and deeper into the dark night of transformation, we often feel a deep resentment, as did Céline, who felt she was being asked to renounce a legitimate pleasure that others could enjoy in peace. This temptation to blasphemy plays itself out in a thousand ways in daily life.

For example, several years ago I had to face the fact that my consumption of alcohol was becoming a real problem in my life. Not only was I overindulging in drinking wine with my evening meal, but I was also beginning to drink in my room after supper. When I finally came to grips with my problem and curtailed my consumption of alcohol, I knew that this was what God was asking me to do. But at the same time, I felt resentment toward people who could freely enjoy this legitimate pleasure. My resentment was irrational because the appetite I was being called to mortify was inordinate. This is an example of how a "blasphemous spirit" is projected as resentment upon others.

Perhaps the best way to understand the temptation to blaspheme God is to regard it as a part of the cross that we have to endure in the dark night of transformation. As we choose to remain steadfast in doing God's will, we must also endure the anger that "it's not fair." By doing so, God's grace heals us of the envy and resentment that are rooted in comparing our lot in life with others. As this healing takes place, we grow in the capacity to "live in the monastery [or family or workplace] as though no one else were in it" (Co 2), that is, we grow in what John calls "spiritual solitude," which is the capacity to rest in God's presence (C 35).

THE SPIRIT OF CONFUSION

Sometimes another loathsome spirit, which Isaiah calls *spiritus vertiginis* [Is 19:14], is sent to these souls, not for their downfall, but to try them. This spirit so darkens the senses that such souls are filled with a thousand scruples and perplexities, so intricate that such persons can never be content with anything, nor can their judgment receive the support of any counsel or idea. This is one of the most burdensome goads and horrors of this night—very similar to what occurs in the spiritual night. (N 1.14.3)

In order to understand this trial, we must first attempt to get a feel for the state of mind that John is describing. He tells us that the core of this trial is that the "senses" (*sentido*) are darkened. Within the context of this passage, *sentido* is best rendered as judgment. In short, these people cannot come to any resolution regarding a decision in their lives because their judgment is "darkened." Things are not clear; they are obscure.

So what is the cause of the obscurity? We should not try to pinpoint a single reason because there may be several. We will explore one possible scenario. However, before doing so, it is important to situate this scenario within John's teaching on faith. This is because faith is the means by which God guides people who are being led into the dark night of the spirit.

The Experience of Faith

Faith is a mode of knowledge, not merely information about God. "Faith . . . gives and communicates God himself to us" (C 12.4). This self-communication of God does not come to us in the form of clear and distinct ideas. Faith is an intuitive mode of apprehension. Or as John puts it, though faith "brings certitude it does not produce clarity" (A 2.6.2). The knowledge that faith provides can be compared to peripheral vision. We are certain that we see something out of the corner of our eye, but what we see is not clear.

The certain and obscure knowledge that faith provides is the precondition of the "spirit of confusion," for doubt is inherent in the very structure of faith. As Paul Tillich writes, "If doubt appears, it should not be considered as a negation of faith, but as an intrinsic element which always and will always be present in active faith."[8] Doubt is always present in an act of faith because it is a choice to trust a Presence that cannot clearly be apprehended.

There are two reasons faith gives rise to doubt. First, the fear engendered in us when we take the risk of stepping out into the unknown triggers a thousand logical reasons we should not venture forth (it is being too rash, it is being presumptuous, etc.). Second, the light that faith imparts overwhelms the light of reason (A 2.3.1) and sometimes calls into question both our worldview and how we interpret reality. This can throw us into a state of confusion in which we are uncertain about what is right and what is wrong. Let us explore the following scenario.

Developmental Scrupulosity

There is an incident in Mark Twain's novel *The Adventures of Huckleberry Finn* that illustrates God's light breaking into our lives. In Twain's story, Huck is helping Jim, a runaway slave, to escape to freedom. However, the night before they anticipate that their raft will arrive at Cairo, Illinois, where they plan to board a steamboat down the Ohio to the Free States, Huck has qualms of conscience. He feels guilty because it dawns on him that what he is doing is wrong.

> I begun to get it through my head that he *was* most free and who was to blame for it? Why *me*. I couldn't get that out of my conscience, no how nor no way. It got to troubling me so I couldn't rest; I couldn't stay still in one place . . . tried to make out to myself that *I* warn't to blame, because *I* didn't run Jim off from his rightful owner; but it warn't no use, conscience up and says, every time, "But you knowed he was running for his freedom, and you could 'a' paddled ashore and told somebody."[9]

Yet, there is still time to right this wrong. Huck climbs into a canoe to turn Jim in, telling Jim that he is just going up the river a piece to ascertain their location. Once on the river, Huck encounters two men in a skiff looking for runaway slaves. When they ask Huck if he has seen any runaway slaves, he lies to the men. Something inside Huck tells him that it would be wrong to hand over a friend. It is beginning to dawn on Huck that Jim is more than what his culture has told him; he's not just a slave but a human being. However, his decision not to hand Jim over doesn't bring Huck peace. He feels guilty because he hasn't done the "right thing." However, he knows that if he did hand Jim over, he would also feel guilty.

"They went off and I got aboard the raft, feeling bad and low, because I knowed very well I had done wrong. . . . Then I thought for a minute, and says to myself, hold on; s'pose you'd 'a' done right and give Jim up, would you felt better than what you do now? No, says I, I'd feel bad—I'd feel just the same way I do now. . . . I was stuck."[10] Huck's anguished dialogue with himself mirrors the state of souls that John describes: souls so "filled with a thousand scruples and perplexities so intricate that [they] can never be content with anything, nor can their judgment receive the support of any counsel or idea" (N 1.14.3). Huck cannot find peace with either decision, no matter what he does. He isn't at home with himself, or as John puts it, "There is no room for [the soul] within itself" (N 2.11.6).

Huck's dilemma may best be labeled as what psychologist Joseph Ciarrocchi calls *developmental scrupulosity*, which is the result of a "newly emerging sense of conscience."[11] Since Huck grew up in a culture that told him slavery was not evil and people had a right to own slaves, he would naturally feel guilty when he believed he was violating the rights of a slave owner. However, when this ingested belief clashes with his growing sense of conscience, Huck is thrown into confusion. He is torn and suspended between two worlds: one dying, the other laboring to be born. What makes Huck's struggle so painful is that all he wants is to do the right thing, but he isn't sure what that is. This is often the situation in which the souls that John is referring to in this chapter find themselves. Let's take another example.

Jeff is forty-five and is employed as an editor at a leading publishing house. Besides being professional in his work, he is good natured, generous with his time, affable, and super responsible. His coworkers have come to depend upon him greatly. He's always on top of things, takes up the slack whenever it is needed, and is the only one in the office who has both the patience and willingness to mentor new employees.

Jeff was raised Catholic, a faith that has always meant a great deal to him. He attends daily Mass before going to work, and five years ago he joined the Secular Order of Discalced Carmelites. His fidelity to daily meditation has made Jeff grow in both self-knowledge and an awareness that God is calling him to participate in various ministries in his parish.

As a result of these new commitments, Jeff has less time and energy to give to colleagues at work. Though he is still both diligent in his work and generous with his time, he is no longer available to jump into the breach and take up the slack as was his custom.

These changes have been difficult for Jeff. Sometimes he can't get to sleep at night because he is afraid his colleagues think he is becoming selfish. However, this isn't his greatest fear. He wonders if he really is becoming selfish. Jeff has come to recognize that his indiscriminate generosity is rooted in his wish to please others and allay his fear of their disapproval. His spiritual director has pointed out to him that bearing the fear of what other people think of him, as he continues to do what he believes is God's calling in his life, is part of the cross he must bear. Jeff believes what his director says is true. He even knows that the guilt he feels when he says "no" to a request made by one of his colleagues is not the result of disregarding God's voice but a reaction of his punishing superego; yet, Jeff is still not sure he is doing the right thing.

Jeff is in the process of developing what is called a "delicate" or "tender" conscience. Under the influence of grace, a person can become sensitive and highly attuned to what is and what is not of God's will. A similar condition is found in David Fleming's interpretation of St. Ignatius's notes concerning scruples. "In the spiritual life, there can be a true awakening of conscience to a wholly new delicacy of conscience. . . . Properly speaking, the temporary lack of certitude and firmness of judgment aroused by this experience is not scrupulosity. Instead, this is recognized traditionally as a symptom of growth. . . . We desire to move beyond the now-recognized dullness or obtuseness of our conscience because we are roused by a new sensitivity of love."[12]

In spite of, or maybe because, of such growth, individuals sometimes find themselves in periods of transition in which there is great confusion. They are plagued by inner doubts, which always seem to be whispering, "But are you really sure?" They cannot come to peace with any choice. So what should we do at such times?

First, we should keep in mind that God is leading us in the darkness and that this trial, like the other two trials (temptations to fornication and blasphemy), is not for our downfall but for our advancement. "So that thus chastised and buffeted, the senses and faculties may gradually be exercised, prepared, and inured for the union with wisdom" (N 1.14.4). In the process, we are being prepared to enter into a deeper reliance upon

God's guidance as we are being detached from our dependence upon the senses for knowledge. In a word, we have to learn to trust God, and trust can only grow by trusting. This is done by choosing to do what we have come to believe is God's will, while we patiently endure the cross of self-doubt.

As we bravely endure the three temptations that John mentions in this chapter, we grow in the strength necessary to transverse the dark night of the spirit.

For Reflection

In this chapter, John has helped us to see that the trials and temptations the dark night brings into our lives are not for our downfall but for our sanctification.

How can this perspective help you to understand your struggles in the spiritual life?

BOOK
TWO

NIGHT 2.1–3

The One Dark Night

⌒⌒⌒

> If His Majesty intends to lead the soul on, he does not put it
> in this dark night of spirit immediately after its going out from
> the aridities and trials of the first purgation and night of sense.
> Instead, after having emerged from the state of beginners, the
> soul usually spends many years exercising itself in the state of
> proficients. . . . The soul readily finds in its spirit, without
> the work of meditation, a very serene, loving contemplation
> and spiritual delight. (N 2.1.1)

This passage can give the erroneous impression that there
is a long period of calm and serenity between two periods
of transformation (the passive night of sense and the passive
night of the spirit), similar to years of peace between two wars.
However, this is not the case. John describes it as a time when
"certain needs [*necesiadades*], aridities [*sequedades*], darknesses
[*tinieblas*], and conflicts [*aprietos*] are felt" (N 2.1.1).

Necesiadades can refer to both our physical and our
emotional needs, wants and drives that are always exerting themselves in our lives. *Sequedades* can refer to either
the emotional doldrums of daily life or a lack of spiritual
fervor. *Tinieblas* can be translated as darkness or obscurity;
it refers to a state of uncertainty, vagueness, or ambiguity.

Aprietos can refer to normal conflicts, difficulties, stresses, or awkward situations.

In short, John is describing the struggles and trials of daily life that we all experience. However, those who are gifted with contemplation relate to these realities from a spiritual perspective. This is because contemplation is the "inflow of God . . . that instructs [us] in the perfection of love" (N 2.5.1). In short, these people are attuned to the choices that God is asking them to make in the midst of their needs, aridities, darknesses, and conflicts. For example, they keep a vigilant guard over their sensual appetites and struggle to remain faithful to their religious obligations during times of aridity. In times of darkness, when God's will is unclear, they are concerned with and often anguish over what they should do. "Am I supposed to say something to this person or keep silent?" "Am I being too rigid or too lenient?" In addition, since contemplation makes them more conscious of the demands of charity, they are put in conflict with their own selfishness.

John is not describing a respite *outside* of the dark night. Rather, it is a continuation of the dark night, which takes place after we have emerged from the initial confusion of the night of sense and before we are plunged into the passive night of the spirit.

During this time, we walk a long road of self-knowledge and gradual transformation as we grow in the virtues. This is what John means when he writes that a soul spends years "exercising itself in the state of proficients" (N 2.1.1). The strength gained during these years is a necessary preparation to enter the passive night of the spirit. "This was the purpose of the reformation of the first night and the calm that resulted from it: that the sensory part, united in a certain way with the spirit, might undergo purgation and suffering with greater fortitude" (N 2.3.2).

In the opening chapters of book two of *The Dark Night*, John underscores the seamless nature of the *one* dark night. He reminds us that the human person, composed of sense and spirit "form[s] only one *suppositum*" (N 2.1.1). We are unified creatures of two interrelated parts. Thus, we can think of the dark night as a single process of purgation that takes place on different levels of our being.

John symbolizes the unity of this process by means of two images. First, "the difference between the two purgations is like the difference between pulling up roots or cutting off a branch" (N 2.2.1). The night of sense prunes the behavioral branches of our inordinate appetites. The night of the spirit digs out the psychic roots of our inordinate appetites from which the branches derive their strength. Second, it is the difference between "rubbing out a fresh stain or an old, deeply embedded one" (N 2.2.1). The night of sense cleanses a stain from the surface of a piece of wood, whereas the night of the spirit lifts out the stain that is deeply embedded in the grain. Both images connote a single process of purification that takes place on deeper and deeper levels of our being. So what is the difference between the passive night of sense and the passive night of the spirit, and how do those two differ from this interval "between" the two nights? In one sense, there is no difference; the purgation is a difference of degree and intensification and not of kind. There is only one night, and in the night of the spirit "both parts are jointly purified" (N 2.3.1).

SAME TEMPTATION, DIFFERENT FORM

John presents us with an example of the unity of the dark night in the area of temptation. Just as beginners are tempted to pride because of their egocentric interpretation of consolation, so too proficients are tempted to pride when they receive imaginative and spiritual visions. "It is here that the devil customarily fills them with presumption and pride. Drawn by vanity and arrogance, they allow themselves to be seen in exterior acts of apparent holiness, such as raptures and other exhibitions. They become audacious with God and lose holy fear, which is the key to and guardian of all the virtues." (N 2.2.3)

The capital sin of pride, like all the capital sins, is a deep inclination toward sinful behavior that is rooted in the spirit. Thus, even though a particular manifestation of a capital sin has been overcome, the inclination has not necessarily been eliminated. To use John's image, even though a particular branch of a tree has been pruned, the roots remain. "All the imperfections and disorders of the sensory part [of the soul] are rooted in the spirit and from it receive their strength. . . . And until these habits are purged, the senses cannot be completely purified of their rebellions and vices" (N 2.3.1).

For Reflection

What are the "needs, aridities, darknesses, and conflicts" (N 2.1.1) that are part and parcel of your daily life?

How has God instructed you to love in the midst of them?

NIGHT 2.4

The Impact of Contemplation

The focus of this very short chapter is how the dark night so transforms the intellect and the will that we don't even recognize ourselves. "I went out from myself. That is, I departed from my low manner of understanding, and my feeble way of loving" (N 2.4.1). This transformation takes place in the interplay between our understanding and our loving, between our perception of reality and our desires. We can only love what we know, but what we love shapes our perception of reality. As Carmelite scholar Hein Blommestijn writes, commenting upon the relationship between desire and perception in the works of St. John of the Cross, "We have the mistaken impression that we experience contact with the reality surrounding us. . . . [However] our perception of reality and our reaction to it are dependent on our needs and desires."[1]

This truth is symbolized in a short story by C. S. Lewis titled "The Shoddy Lands." The story begins as an unnamed Oxford don receives a phone call from a former student, named Durward. He tells the professor that he is passing through Oxford and would like to drop in for a visit. The professor is delighted at the prospect of having a tête-à-tête with

Durward. However, he becomes frustrated when Durward arrives with Peggy, his fiancée.

It was an awkward situation at first. The professor and Durward could not talk about their mutual interests, for that would leave Peggy out of the conversation. Likewise, Durward and Peggy felt it would be rude to focus the conversation upon their relationship because that would exclude the professor from the conversation. So the three of them just sat and talked about the weather and the news.

As they were talking, the professor became bored and began to stare at Peggy. Quite suddenly, his office vanished; Durward and Peggy vanished, and he found himself alone in a strange rural setting that he described as "nondescript and shoddy."[2]

Everything—the trees, the sky, and the grass—were all blurry and dingy green. The only things that were clear and vivid were certain flowers, such as daffodils and roses. The professor felt that apart from the daffodils and roses, he "had suddenly been banished from the real, bright, concrete, and prodigally complex world into some sort of second-rate universe that had been put together on the cheap."[3]

As the professor surveyed this strange place, he saw a silvery light in the distance and began to walk toward it. It led him into a city where he encountered a crowd of indistinct "Walking Things." He noticed that the silvery light proceeded from selected store windows—those that exhibited jewelry, women's shoes, and clothing. Like the daffodils and roses in the countryside, they were the only objects that were clear and vivid.

As he continued to walk, he encountered what, at first, seemed like a large building but discovered that it was an immense woman. She was lying, practically naked, on a sunlit beach and looked like a model in an advertisement for women's swimwear. When he looked into the women's eyes, he recognized her as Peggy. Suddenly, the professor found himself back in his office with Durward and Peggy. When they left, the professor pondered his strange experience and came to the following explanation.

> My view is that by the operation of some unknown psychological, or pathological, law, I was, for a second or so, let into Peggy's mind; at least to the extent of seeing her world, the world as it exists for her. At the centre of that world is a swollen image of herself, remodelled to be as like the girls in the advertisements as possible. Round this are grouped clear and distinct images of the things she really cares about. Beyond that, the whole earth and sky are a vague blur. The daffodils and roses are especially instructive. Flowers only exist for her if they are the sort that can be cut and put in vases or sent as bouquets; flowers in themselves, flowers as you see them in the woods, are negligible.[4]

All of us are implicated in this story. What our minds select to focus on and ignore is regulated by our desires. Our mental radar is finely attuned to perceive things in our environment that we value, and to tune out objects that we deem unimportant. Our mental energy is often absorbed by our egocentric preoccupations and is withdrawn from objects that we consider being of no consequence.

However, in the dark night, under the influence of contemplation, as our desires are purified our perceptions are transformed. We "understand . . . by means of divine wisdom" (N 2.4.2) because we have departed from our "feeble way of loving" (N 2.4.1). For, "where there is love there is vision," as St. Thomas Aquinas teaches (*The Sentences*, III, 35, I, 2).

For Reflection

Do you want to "understand . . . by means of divine wisdom" (N 2.4.2)? Think before you answer. If you receive God's wisdom, you will perceive how "feeble [is] your way of loving" (N 2.4.1). Then you will have to make a decision either to act upon what God has revealed to you or to ignore God's invitation to love.

NIGHT 2.5–6

Illumination and Purgation

~⌒~

> This dark night is an inflow [*influencia*] of God into the soul, which purges it of its habitual ignorances and imperfections, natural and spiritual, and which the contemplatives call infused contemplation or mystical theology. Through this contemplation, God teaches the soul secretly and instructs it in the perfection of love without its doing anything or understanding how this happens. (N 2.5.1)

T he dark night is the *influencia*, that is, the influence or impact that the presence of God exerts upon us in the process of spiritual transformation. In the above passage, John subsumes the various ways that grace impacts us under two overarching categories: illumination and purgation.

ILLUMINATION

There often exists within us an obstinate blindness that resists God's light. It is a "vicious darkness" (F 1.22), which reacts like a cornered animal. When God reveals to us the truth of our lives, we feel threatened and go on the attack with every rationalization in our arsenal. The darkness is tenacious and clings to "attachments one never really desires to conquer" (A

1.11.4). When God's light shines within the depths of our souls, we realize that we are a dark wood of ignorance and sin. We have become entangled in a wood that Dante describes as being "savage, dense and harsh" (*Inferno* 1.5). Our resistance to the light is savage because our "habitual ignorances" are willful. We do not want to see because we do not want to change.

Reflection, prayer, or psychoanalysis cannot impart the self-knowledge that the dark night of the spirit imparts, although these may assist the process. Our inner darkness can be so deep and our resistance to seeing the truth of our lives so fierce that only God can accomplish this task. "It is impossible to perceive one's darknesses without the divine light focusing on them" (F 1.22).

One might think that because "contemplation is the loving wisdom of God" (N 2.5.1) that the divine inflow would ravish us with delight. However, the opposite is often true; we often experience "affliction and torment" (N 2.5.2). This is because we see not the light but only what the light discloses. Divine grace that flows into us can be likened to a ray of light that shines through a slat into a darkened room by which we see specks of dust floating in the air. "The soul, because of its impurity, suffers immensely at the time this divine light truly assails it . . . beholding its impurity by means of this pure light. . . . This divine and dark light causes deep immersion of the mind in the knowledge and feeling of one's own miseries and evils; it brings all these miseries into relief" (N 2.5.5).[1]

We cannot experience the true nature of the divine inflow because we are immersed and engulfed in the consciousness of our sinfulness. As our darkness becomes visible, we are overwhelmed by guilt. In consequence, we "feel so unclean and wretched that it seems that God is against [us]" (N 2.5.5). We believe that God is harsh and pitiless. "Individuals feel so far from all favor that they think . . . that no one will take pity on them. How amazing and pitiful it is that the soul be so utterly weak and impure that the hand of God, though light and gentle, should feel so heavy and contrary. For the hand of God does not press down or weigh the soul, but only touches it; and this mercifully, for God's aim is to grant it favors and not to chastise it" (N 2.5.7).

When we look at God through the lens of guilt, mercy feels like wrath. When we project the fear of chastisement upon God's loving countenance, we feel we have been cast outside of God's favor. In our wretchedness we can believe that God's hand is poised to strike, when it is raised in blessing. It is only at the end of Francis Thompson's poem "The Hound of Heaven" that the protagonist discovers his fear was unfounded because his perception was distorted. God was pursuing him not like some vicious hound in order to devour him but to pardon and heal him. "Is my gloom after all, Shade of His hand outstretched caressingly?"[2] Or as John puts it, "For the hand of God does not press down or weigh the soul, but only touches it; and this mercifully, for God's aim is to grant it favors and not to chastise it" (N 2.5.7). When our mind is submerged in the dark night, we cannot perceive God's loving countenance, for we project our sinfulness and guilt upon God's face. "We are consumed by your anger; by your wrath we are overwhelmed. You have set our iniquities before us, our secret sins in the light of your countenance" (Ps 90:7–8). The illumination that the dark night engenders is painful but necessary. As English novelist and poet Thomas Hardy wrote, "If way to the Better there be, it exacts a full look at the Worst."[3]

PURGATION

The divine inflow not only "calls us out of darkness" but also leads us "into his own marvelous light" (1Pt 2:9) by instructing us "in the perfection of love" (N 2.5.1). Love beckons us to leave our old way of life behind, or, to use John's metaphor, "to leave home." This is an excruciatingly painful process. The dark night is "an oppressive undoing" (N 2.6.5). It unravels the deeply woven patterns of our behavior that constitute the warp and woof of daily life.

God invites us to grow beyond the narrow confines of our insular, self-willed existence. Consequently, this loving invitation is experienced not as a gentle presence but as an alien being who intrudes upon our settled lives. Just as we experience not the divine light that shines upon us but only our own inner darkness, so too do we experience not God's loving invitation but only our resistance. "This flame [of God's presence] of itself is extremely loving [but] the will of itself is excessively dry [*seca*] and hard [*dura*]. . . . Because this flame is immense and far-reaching, and the will is narrow and restricted, the will feels its confinement and narrowness in the measure that the flame attacks. It feels this until the flame, penetrating within it, enlarges, widens, and makes it capable of receiving the flame itself" (F 1.23).

In the presence of love itself, we realize how deep is our resistance to change and how small we have become. *Dura* means to last, to continue, to endure, and when used negatively, as it is in this passage, to what is resistant to change, what has become unyielding, inflexible, and impenetrable. *Seca* means to be dried up, withered, or shrunken. Indeed, we have become small and shriveled to the extent that we cannot love.

Thus, as God awakens our desire to live a more expansive life, we become painfully aware of the cramped cell in which we are imprisoned. How thick its walls and how obdurate and deaf we have become to love's entreaties. This painful realization plunges us into deep guilt and regret, and we are overwhelmed at what we have become.

Just as self-knowledge is painful, so too is change. And the change native to the dark night is excruciatingly painful because it involves modifying or eradicating deeply ingrained habits that have taken root within us over a lifetime. "This contemplation annihilates empties and consumes all the affections and impure habits the soul contracted throughout its life" (N 2.6.5). It is "an oppressive undoing" (N 2.6.5), "a terrible undoing" (N 2.6.6) by which the patterns of our lives are unraveled, "disentangle[d]," and "dissolve[d]" (N 2.6.1).

When a deeply rooted habit is undone or disentangled, the experience can be so painful that it can be compared to the ripping and tearing away of our flesh. "[She] was ripped from my side. So deeply was she engrafted into my heart that it was left torn and wounded and trailing with blood."[4] Thus is St. Augustine's description of his heartrending decision to separate from his common-law wife whom he loved deeply. Any ingrained behavior in our life may be a major barrier to growing in love and a serious roadblock on the spiritual path. In this regard, it is instructive to consider some of the specific examples of habitual imperfections that are mentioned by John.

> Some examples of these habitual imperfections are: the common habit of being very talkative; a small attachment one never really desires to conquer, for example, to a person, to clothing, to a book or a cell, or to the way food is prepared,

and to other trifling conversations and little satisfactions in tasting, knowing, and hearing things, and so on. Any of these habitual imperfections to which there is attachment is as harmful to progress in virtue as the daily commission of many other imperfections and sporadic venial sins that do not result from a bad habit. These latter will not hinder a person as much as will the attachment to something. As long as this attachment remains, it is impossible to make progress in perfection, even though the imperfection may be very small (A 1.11.4).

John's list may seem to consist of trifles. However, these are precisely the objects and behaviors that imperceptibly become deeply woven into the pattern of our daily lives and are highly resistant to change. They are the routines that become ruts, in which we've become so deeply entrenched that we have neither the energy nor the inclination to climb out of them. They are the habits that we "never really desire to conquer" (A 1.11.4).

A desire that is not a real desire is worse than a sham; it is a subtle form of self-deception. When we feel a desire to change we can believe we are trying to change, even when we do not exert any effort to do so. The sophistic logic goes something like the following: if I feel a desire to change, then I'm struggling to change. We can live under the delusion that feeling is willing.

We can feed ourselves untruths for so long that we no longer realize we are lying to ourselves. When our rationalizations become deeply rooted in our minds, we are no longer aware of our self-deception. As St. Augustine writes of his own avoidance of God, "I had grown used to pretending that the only reason why I had not yet turned my back on the world to serve you [my God] was that my perception of the truth was uncertain, but that excuse was no longer available to me."[5]

However, even when Augustine broke through his rationalizations, he equivocated. "I had no answer to give as you said to me, *Arise, sleeper, rise from the dead: Christ will enlighten you* . . . [except] 'just a minute,' 'One more minute,' 'Let me have a little longer.' But these 'minutes' never diminished, and my 'little longer' lasted inordinately long."[6]

Like Augustine, when we never really desire to conquer something, we will use any device at our disposal to procrastinate. However, the inflow of God's love is stronger and more persistent than our resistance. Love pursues us relentlessly "with unhurrying chase and unperturbed pace."[7]

For Reflection

Is there a "common habit" or a "small attachment" (A 1.11.4) in your life that you have "never really desire[d] to conquer" (A 1.11.4)? Are you protecting it behind thick walls of rationalization? Like St. Augustine, do you say to God, "Just a minute . . . let me have a little longer"?

NIGHT 2.7

The Straits of the Will

THE CAGED MIND

Think of a time when you violated your conscience and were filled with guilt and weighed down with a feeling of dread.[1] This is similar to what we feel when the "divine and dark night" sears our souls. It causes a "deep immersion of the mind" as God's light throws our "miseries and evils . . . into relief" (N 2.5.5). Our darkness stands in stark relief to God's light because in the dark night "two extremes, divine and human" (N 2.6.1), are being joined together.

In this chapter, John continues to describe the experience of the mind being immersed in the dark night by means of the image of being imprisoned. "[God] has built a fence around me. . . . [God] has made a fence around me . . . that I might not go out. . . . [God] has closed up my exits" (N 2.7.2). I am "imprisoned in a dark dungeon, bound hands and feet" (N 2.7.3).

In the dark night, we feel so "cabined, cribbed and confined" that all hope that we will ever be released from our prison has been squeezed out of our minds. We believe that our "evil will never end" (N 2.7.3) and our "blessings are gone forever" (N 2.7.6). We feel unloved, "despised by creatures, particularly by [our] friends" (N 2.6.3), and "think that God does not love [us] and [that we] are unworthy of his love" (N 2.7.7).

When we are in such a state of soul, we are inconsolable. No one can convince us that what we are going through is for our spiritual welfare. Although our "spiritual director may point out many reasons for comfort on account of the blessings contained in these afflictions, [we] cannot believe this" (N 2.7.3). Since we are "engulfed and immersed in that feeling of evil by which [we] clearly see [our] own miseries" (N 2.7.3), we are unable to see anything else. We interpret the whole of who we are from an emotional perspective, which makes it impossible for us to realize the spiritual transformation that the dark night is accomplishing within us.

HUMBLED AND SOFTENED

Before we are placed in the crucible of the dark night, we are often proud, and we judge people harshly. However, after we emerge from the transforming forge, we are "humbled [and] softened" (N 2.7.3). The self-knowledge that humility bestows does not demean us; it deflates our egos. It does not diminish our worth but softens our glaring self-glorification. Dante presents us with an image of this process in the *Purgatorio*. He describes the Angel of Humility as the light of the morning star that softens at the approach of the light of the sun. Its light does not diminish but softens in the presence of a greater light. "The fair creature, garbed in white, came toward us. In his face there was what seemed the shimmering of the morning star" (*Purgatorio*, canto 12, lines 88–90).[2] So too, in the dark night, our spirit becomes humbled and softened as it stands in the presence of God.

In this chapter, John discloses to us the spiritual transformation that takes place beneath the emotional pain of the
conscious mind. When our mind feels imprisoned, our soul
is being released. When we feel humiliated, our pride is being
humbled, and our harsh judgments are being softened.

THE LUMP OF SIN

In the dark night, the knowledge of our miseries and evils
is experienced in two ways. As the author of *The Cloud of
Unknowing* writes, first we "experience sin as a *lump*, realizing
that it is yourself."[3] We feel en masse all of our ingrained sinful habits that we never really desired to conquer; we become
keenly aware of our deep-seated sloth and mediocrity; we realize how paltry and mercenary is our love and how everything
we do seems to be shot through with pride.

Second, sometimes God's searing light focuses upon a specific sin in our past. Such an experience not only is painful
but also can be problematic. Let's take an example of a married man who, during a rocky time in his marriage, had a brief
affair. He was twenty-five years old at the time. For the next
thirty years, he remained faithful to his wife and lived in a
happy marriage. He became active in his parish and developed
a deep prayer life.

However, at the age of fifty-five, his past love affair began to
prey on his mind. When he looked back at what he had done,
he was filled with deep feelings of guilt and remorse. "How
could I have done this to the woman I love?" At times, the feelings were so intense that he found it difficult to look his wife in
the eye. He felt compelled to tell her about his infidelity.

Let us presuppose that his remorse is the result of the dark
night, an expression of the "afflictions [that] pierce the soul

when it suddenly remembers the evils in which it sees itself immersed" (N 2.7.1). Given this fact, what advice would you offer this man? Should he tell his wife about his affair? What questions would you explore with him?

It might be argued that since the man's feelings of guilt are the direct result of grace, he should trust his feelings and tell his wife about his affair. However, we must remember that any grace of God does not contain its own interpretation. We have already dealt with this distinction. Recall that beginners usually misinterpret the grace of consolation, namely, because they feel holy, they conclude they are holy. Likewise, people who are immersed in the dark night "feel so unclean and wretched that it seems God is against them and they are against God. It seems that God has rejected [them]" (N 2.5.5).

Although the man's feelings of guilt are the direct result of the piercing light of grace, we should not conclude that his interpretation of how he should act is divinely inspired. Given this fact, should this man tell his wife about his affair? I do not have an answer to this question. However, as a spiritual director, I would explore the following questions with the man.

Director: Why do you believe you should tell your wife about your affair?

Man: I'm not sure; I just feel I should. I feel I'm living with a secret, and I want to be open.

Director: Your feelings are understandable, and I think it's admirable that you want to be honest with your wife. However, I think we need to explore the possible consequences of telling her about your affair.

Man: What do you mean?

Director: Well, how would it affect your relationship with your wife? Would it improve it or injure it? Does your wife have the emotional strength to bear your revelation?

Man: I don't know.

Director: Also, you might want to ask yourself for whose sake would you reveal your affair, for your wife's sake or for yours?

Man: What do you mean?

Director: You obviously love your wife, and you want to be honest with her. However, you should ask yourself to what extent your motive to tell her about your affair is being driven by your need to obtain relief from your feelings.

Man: You're right, I really need to think about that.

Our feelings can blind us to the consequences of our choices, even those made with the best of intentions. We have an example of this in Tolstoy's novel *Anna Karenina* that is related to the above dialogue between the man and his director. Konstantin Levin, who is a very good and honest man, feels there must be no secrets between himself and his fiancée Kitty Shtcherbatsky. In consequence of his feelings, he gives her his diary, which chronicles his lecherous past.

> Levin, not without an inner struggle, handed her his diary. He knew that between him and her there could not be, and should not be, secrets, and so he had decided that so it must be. But he had not realized what an effect it would have on her, he had not put himself in her place. It was only when the same evening he came to their house before the theater, went into her room and saw her tear-stained, pitiful, sweet face, miserable with suffering he had caused and nothing could

undo, he felt the abyss that separated his shameful past from her dovelike purity, and was appalled at what he had done.

"Take them, take these dreadful books!" she said, pushing away the notebooks lying before her on the table. "Why did you give them to me? . . . It's awful, awful!"

His head sank, and he was silent. He could say nothing.

"You can't forgive me," he whispered.

"Yes, I forgive you; but it's terrible!"[4]

Levin was an honest man who loved Kitty deeply. Unfortunately, his feelings blinded him to the consequences of his choice to reveal his past. Spiritual discernment is something that has to be taught. As John tells us, "God teaches the soul secretly and instructs it in the perfection of love" (N 1.5.1).

For Reflection

When you feel "that God does not love" you and that you "are unworthy of his love" (N 2.7.7) because your mind is immersed in feelings of your sinfulness, can you also experience the fruit of God's grace operating in your life, namely, that your pride is being humbled and your harsh judgments are being softened?

Have you ever been overwhelmed by a deep sense of guilt regarding a sin or indiscretion that you have committed in your past?

Have you ever considered that your feelings of guilt are the result of the searing light of God's grace?

The Paradoxes of Transformation

> They all go into the dark, the vacant interstellar spaces . . .
> the vacant into the vacant. [They have] lost the motive of
> action . . . [and enter] a silent funeral . . . which is the
> darkness of God.[1]

These words of T. S. Eliot capture the mental and emotional void that often accompanies the dark night, what
St. Thérèse of Lisieux called "the night of nothingness" (S
213). The vacant interstellar spaces are symbols of the mind,
the imagination, and memory that feel empty and barren.
They are wastelands in which the wellsprings of psychic energy
have dried up. All thoughts, images, and memories are black
and white, cardboard, and two-dimensional. Everything feels
dull, drab, and lifeless. We find it extremely difficult to "attend
to temporal affairs and business . . . [and] can neither pray
vocally nor be attentive to spiritual matters" (N 2.8.1).

We feel that the spiritual life has lost a sense of purpose,
has "lost the motive of action." Prayer is reduced to a mechani-
cal exercise, the mouthing of empty words, uttered "with little
strength and fervor" (N 2.8.1). However, what we are unable
to comprehend is that our psychic energy has not dried up;
rather, "contemplation absorbs" it, because our mind, memory,

and will are submerged and "engulfed in [the] divine and dark spiritual light of contemplation" (N 2.8.2).

This is one of the paradoxes of the dark night. When our soul has become submerged in grace, we feel that God is absent. Nevertheless, we still experience God, not in the imagination, the intellect, or the memory but in our desire for God. As St. Thérèse wrote during her dark night, "When I sing of the happiness of heaven and of the eternal possession of God, I feel no joy in this, for I sing simply what I WANT TO BELIEVE" (S 214). In short, Thérèse's belief was in her desire to believe.

Similarly, in the dark night, though we feel that God is absent, God is present in our longing. Though we feel empty and void, our prayer is full of yearning and desire. "The soul does beseech [*ruega*] God" (N 2.8.1). The word *ruega* means a strong expression of desire; it means to implore, to crave, to beg, to plead. "O God, you are my God, I seek you, my soul thirsts for you . . . as in a dry and weary land where there is no water" (Ps 63:1).

When we find ourselves in this state of dry longing, John advises us not to force ourselves to pray but to accept our condition patiently and allow our longing to pray for us. To accept this condition with patience is to do much; it allows the dry contemplation to accomplish its transforming work. "This is not the time to speak to God, but the time to put one's mouth in the dust . . . so that there might come some actual hope [Lam 3:29] and the time to suffer this purgation patiently" (N 2.8.1).

What does it mean to suffer purgation patiently? It means to go on living while suffering a great loss. It is comparable to going back to work after the death of a loved one. While you are inwardly absorbed in your loss, you are required to attend to the outward details of life. The only difference is that you don't feel you have the emotional resources to deal with them.

In the dark night, God provides us with the strength to carry on and even to will, though it knows not how, to accept God's grace and "to suffer this purgation patiently" (N 2.8.1). There are fewer sufferings greater than to attend to the tasks of daily life, while being submerged in the forge of the Divine Blacksmith.

THE DARKNESS THAT IMPARTS LIGHT

> This happy night darkens the spirit . . . only to impart light concerning all things. . . . [This] demands the annihilation and expulsion of the natural affections and apprehensions. . . . That the intellect reach union with the divine light and become divine . . . this dark contemplation must first purge and annihilate it of its natural light and its habitual way of understanding, which was a long time in use, and that divine light and illumination take its place. Since that strength of understanding was natural to the intellect, the darkness it here suffers is profound, frightful, and extremely painful. This darkness seems to be substantial darkness, since it is felt in the deep substance of the spirit. (N 2.9.1–3)

In Plato's *Republic*, Socrates describes men who have been imprisoned in a cave since childhood. Their legs and necks are shackled; they cannot turn their heads; and they can only see the wall that is in front of them. Behind them is a fire. Between the fire and the men is a raised walkway on which various objects are being paraded. The shadows of these objects are projected upon the wall in front of the prisoners. All day long,

THE PARADOXES OF TRANSFORMATION ♦ 155

the prisoners sit and study the shadows, which they regard as reality. An individual is praised if he is able to abstract a scrap of knowledge from a shadow.

Imagine, says Socrates, that a prisoner is released from his chains. He turns around and looks at the fire. The brightness of the fire is so painful that he shuts his eyes. He becomes afraid and is unable to function because he can no longer see his shadows, which for him constitute reality.

Now imagine, says Socrates, after his eyes have adjusted to the light, that he opens them and sees the objects whose shadows are projected upon the wall. When he is told that these objects are reality, he becomes so confused and afraid that he turns back to his shadows that constitute the world of the familiar.

Imagine, says Socrates, that this man is dragged outside the cave and is forced to stand in the bright sunlight. He becomes blinded and disoriented. But as his eyes adjust to the light, his fear gradually subsides as he begins to be enchanted by the new world that he sees. Contemplating the world around him, he understands that the shadows in the cave are merely dim scraps of reality. He stands in wonder as an enchanting three-dimensional universe, filled with a rich variety of form, color, and texture, unfolds before him.

All of us are like the people in Plato's cave. We are chained to the shadows of our minds, which we call "reality." Having defined reality by means of these shadows, we are threatened when the light dissolves them. This is a metaphor of what happens in the dark night. As the "dark contemplation . . . purge[s] and annihilate[s] our habitual way of understanding," our "suffer[ing] is profound, frightful, and extremely painful" (N 2.9.3). Our two-dimensional moral and spiritual world, with its clear-cut categories of right and wrong and our beliefs of how God operates, is thrown into confusion.

Furthermore, the shadows of our mind upon which we construct our identities and personal fictions, and upon which we depend to make sense out of our lives, begin to crumble into uncertainty. We feel a fearful estrangement from ourselves as we lose hold of our old world of understanding. However, in the process, we gradually become enchanted as our eyes adjust to seeing a new world.

> This night withdraws the spirit from its customary manner of experience to bring it to the divine experience that is foreign to every human way. It seems to the soul in this night that it is being carried out of itself by afflictions. At other times the soul wonders if it is not being charmed, and it goes about with wonderment over what it sees and hears. Everything seems very strange even though a person is the same as always. The reason is that the soul is being made a stranger to its usual knowledge and experience of things so that, annihilated in this respect, it may be informed with the divine, which belongs more to the next life than to this. (N 2.9.5)

To understand this passage, we need to remind ourselves that the dark night is divine grace or the presence of God transforming us, or to use John's language, it is "an inflow of God into the soul" (N 2.5.1). John expresses the same truth by saying that we are in the process of being "informed with the divine" (*informada en el divino*).

Being informed does not refer to receiving information. John is most probably using the term *form* in its Scholastic sense, which refers to the actualizing principle of a creature that makes a thing what it is. Being "informed with the divine" does not make us a different creature than what we are; rather, it means we are growing into the creature we are meant to be, in the same way that a seed grows into an oak tree. The dark night is the seed of grace germinating into glory. This is why people who are experiencing transformation "belong more to the next life than to this" (N 2.9.5).

Using the metaphor of sight to express this reality, John writes that these transformed individuals know "creatures through God and not God through creatures. This amounts to knowing the effects through their cause and not the cause through their effects" (F 4.5). It is as if they see the world through the eyes of God. The lenses of their perception have been transformed because their wills have been purified. As William Blake puts it, "If the doors of perception were cleansed, everything would appear to man as it is, infinite."[2]

THE HUMILITY THAT EXALTS

"This happy night . . . humbles individuals and reveals their miseries . . . only to exalt them" (N 2.9.1). After G. K. Chesterton read George Meredith's novel *The Egoist*, he wrote to his fiancée Frances and expressed how much he pitied Meredith's protagonist because "he never experienced the splendid and exalting sensation of being unnecessary."[3]

Chesterton is not saying that we are unimportant but that we are not indispensable. It is a humbling experience when we realize that the world can get along without us. However, it is a realization that exalts us, for we become buoyant when we are relieved of the crushing burden of taking ourselves too seriously. In *The Pickwick Papers*, Charles Dickens gives us an image of the lightness of being which humility bestows. "It was the sort of afternoon that might induce a couple of elderly gentlemen, in a lonely field, to take off their great-coats and play leap-frog in pure lightness of heart and gaiety."[4]

The dark night elevates us by stripping us of what weighs us down—the "great-coats" of our pride. "Truly I tell you, unless you change and become like little children, you will never enter the kingdom of heaven" (Mt 18:3).

THE POVERTY THAT ENRICHES

"This happy night . . . impoverishes and empties them of all possessions and natural affection . . . only that they may reach [*extender*] out divinely [*divinamente*] to the enjoyment [*gozar*] of all earthly and heavenly things, with a general freedom of spirit in them all" (N 2.9.1).

The root word for happy is derived from the Middle English *hap*, meaning an occurrence or what is happening. In short, the scope of our happiness is determined by our capacity to be present to what is happening. This is the fruit of detachment. As the sixth-century monk Dorotheus of Gaza writes, detachment is "being free from [wanting] certain things to happen [and] what is happening will be the thing you want and you will be at peace with all."[5]

As we are transformed and purified, our capacity to enjoy all things expands. We are able to *extender*, that is, to extend, to reach out, and to expand our range of enjoyment, because we are able to let things just be. Having been released from the clutches of a grasping, manipulating, exploitative stance before life, we are able to "obtain more joy and recreation in creatures" (A 3.20.2). This is because for "those whose joy is unpossessive of things [they are able to] rejoice in them all as though they possessed them all" (A 3.20.3).

We have a symbol of a nonpossessive heart that possesses all things in the enigmatic character of Tom Bombadil, in J. R. R. Tolkien's trilogy, *The Lord of the Rings*. Tom Bombadil, who is "fatherless,"[6] has frequently been compared to Adam before the Fall. When Frodo asks Goldberry who Tom Bombadil is, she replies that he is "the Master of wood, water, and hill." "'Then all this strange land belongs to him?' replies Frodo. Goldberry responds, 'No, indeed. . . . That would be a burden . . . the trees and the grasses and all things growing or living in the land belong each to themselves.'"[7]

The paradox of Tom Bombadil's mastery over creation lies in the fact that he does not want to possess anything. In consequence, he is the only character in *The Lord of the Rings* who is immune to the corrupting influence of the One Ring of Power. He treats the ring as a plaything. He slips the ring onto his finger with no ill effects because he does not desire to possess what the ring offers.[8] The paradox of the nonpossessive heart is that it is able to possess all things. Thus, it can sing with exultation, "Mine are the heavens and mine is the earth. Mine are the nations, the just are mine, and mine are sinners. The angels are mine, and the Mother of God, and all things are mine; and God himself is mine and for me, because Christ is mine and all for me" (SLL 27).

The nonpossessive soul is the master of all that exists because it does not desire to possess anything. In consequence, it can "rejoice in them all as though they possessed them all" (A 3.20.3).

SPIRITUAL JOY

In addition to the vast scope of the joy that is experienced by nonpossessive people, the nature of their joy is qualitatively different from those who are in the grip of possessiveness. They "reach out divinely [*divinamente*]" (N 2.9.1). John expounds upon this capacity to perceive reality "divinely" by means of what he calls the "spiritual senses."

The concept of the "spiritual senses" is a way of positing that the more we become united to God, the more our capacity to perceive reality increases. The more we are transformed by grace, the more we participate in the way that God perceives reality. Using the sense of sight by way of example, it is as if John is saying that when we are united to God, we are able to see through the eyes of God. "The soul knows creatures through God and not God through creatures. This amounts to knowing the effects through their cause and not the cause through its effects" (F 4.5).

Although these words are written by way of analogy, they should not be taken as mere metaphor. For when we become "refined and inured, [our] eyes by which [we] now view these things will be as different from those of the past as is spirit from sense and divine from human" (N 2.9.5). We find an example of this in the life of the Trappist monk Thomas Merton who, by grace, was able to shed a restricted concept of holiness that blinded him to seeing as God sees. He writes,

> In Louisville, at the corner of Fourth and Walnut . . . I was suddenly overwhelmed with the realization that I loved all those people, that they were mine and I theirs, that we could not be alien to one another even though we were total strangers. It was like waking from a dream of separateness, of spurious self-isolation in a special world, the world of renunciation and supposed holiness. The whole illusion of a separate holy existence is a dream. . . . The concept of "separation from the world" that we have in the monastery too easily presents itself as a complete illusion: the illusion that by making vows we become a different species of being. . . . To think that

for sixteen or seventeen years I have been taking seriously this pure illusion that is implicit in so much of our monastic thinking. . . .

Then it was as if I suddenly saw the secret beauty of their hearts, the depths of their hearts where neither sin nor desire nor self-knowledge can reach, the core of their reality, the person that each one is in God's eyes.[9]

As the dark night purifies our sight and quiets our inordinate appetites, our capacity to perceive deepens. As William Wordsworth puts it, "With an eye made quiet by the power of harmony and the deep power of joy, we see into the life of things."[10]

When we are able to see into the life of things, or "penetrate the truth and value of things" (A 3.20.2), our joy becomes as deep as our perception. We no longer feed on the surface of life but feast at its core, for we are able to "delight in the substance of [things]" (A 3.20.2).

For Reflection

Pride can infect us with what Samuel Johnson calls "the fever of renown,"[11] the desperate need to acquire a privileged position in the minds of others. "Pride is the downward drag of all things into . . . selfish seriousness," by which "Satan fell by the force of gravity," wrote G. K. Chesterton.[12] How accurately these words describe one of the chief effects of pride. It weighs us down under the burden of taking ourselves too seriously and exhausts us in our pursuit of some claim to fame.

CONTINUED

One of the great graces of the dark night is that it "reveals [our] miseries" to us (N 2.9.1). It makes us painfully aware of the great burden that pride makes us carry and engenders a desire to stop our mad pursuit.

Is God inviting you to lay down your burden through sheer exhaustion?

NIGHT 2.10

The Burning Log

For the sake of further clarity in this matter, we ought to note that this purgative and loving knowledge, or divine light we are speaking of, has the same effect on a soul that fire has on a log of wood. The soul is purged and prepared for union with the divine light just as the wood is prepared for transformation into the fire. Fire, when applied to wood, first dehumidifies it, dispelling all moisture and making it give off any water it contains. Then it gradually turns the wood black, makes it dark and ugly, and even causes it to emit a bad odor. By drying out the wood, the fire brings to light and expels all those ugly and dark accidents that are contrary to fire. Finally, by heating and enkindling it from without, the fire transforms the wood into itself and makes it as beautiful as it is itself. Once transformed, the wood no longer has any activity or passivity of its own, except for its weight and its quantity that is denser than the fire. It possesses the properties and performs the actions of fire: It is dry and it dries; it is hot and it gives off heat; it is brilliant and it illumines; it is also much lighter in weight than before. It is the fire that produces all these properties in the wood. (N 2.10.1)

I magine John teaching a college course on the dark night. After covering a substantial amount of material, he wants to summarize what he has taught thus far and point to the material that he will cover for the remainder of the course. This is analogous to what John does with his image of the burning log.

Up to this chapter, John has focused on the purgative aspect of the dark night. In the next chapter, he will begin his treatment of the transformative aspects of the dark night. The image of the burning log touches upon the salient points of both the purgative and the transformative aspects of the dark night. Let us look at each in turn.

THE DARK NIGHT

The image of the burning log is a symbol of the nature of the dark night. It is not a spiritual program that we design; it is the presence of God purifying and transforming the soul. It is neither abstract nor arbitrary; it is inseparable from our personal histories. "[It] consumes all the affections and imperfect habits the soul contracted throughout its life" (N 2.6.5). The dark night is an "oppressive undoing" (N 2.6.5), a "terrible undoing" (N 2.6.6) that "brings to light and expels all those ugly and dark accidents that are contrary to fire" (N 2.10.1).

Though God brings to light the unconverted parts of our souls, we should not think that he does so apart from the events of daily life. In fact, God sometimes uses an event as ordinary as walking down a street as the instrument of our enlightenment. Let us look at an example from the life of St. Augustine.

In 384, St. Augustine had just been appointed a professor of rhetoric in Milan, where the imperial court resided. Through influential friends, he was commissioned to deliver the official panegyric to the emperor at court. One day, as Augustine was in the process of preparing his oration of empty flattery, he was walking down a street in Milan and saw a drunken beggar.

> I recall how miserable I was, and how one day you brought me to a realization of my miserable state. I was preparing to deliver a eulogy upon the emperor in which I would tell plenty of lies with the object of winning favor with the well-informed by my lying. . . . As I passed through a certain district in Milan I noticed a poor beggar, drunk and making merry. . . . Goaded with greed, I was dragging my load of unhappiness along, and feeling it all the heavier for being dragged. . . . With the help of a few paltry coins he had collected by begging this man was enjoying the temporal happiness for which I strove by so bitter, devious and roundabout a contrivance. His joy was no true joy, to be sure, but what I was seeking in my ambition was a joy far more unreal. . . . He was happier, not only inasmuch as he was flooded with merriment while I was torn with cares, but also because he has earned his wine by wishing good-day to passers-by, while I was seeking a swollen reputation by lying.[1]

John writes that the dark night "stirs up [*removiendo*] all the foul and vicious humors of which the soul was never before aware" (N 2.10.2). *Removiendo* can be rendered as simply "remove," or it can be translated as the "fermentation of the humors." Though John may not have had this latter meaning in mind, it accurately describes a dark night experience in which God uses the events of our lives as a catalyst that stirs up, ferments, and agitates the soul and makes it conscious of its own misery.

In this regard, we can interpret Augustine's encounter with the drunken beggar as a dark night experience. Though

Augustine was somewhat aware of his misery, God brought it to a head. "I recall how miserable I was, and how one day you brought me to a realization of my miserable state." This was a pivotal event in Augustine's life; it happened just prior to his conversion in the garden.[2]

The important truth contained in this incident is that the grace of the dark night operates within the concrete reality of our lives; God uses events, sights, and sounds to enlighten us to our "habitual ignorances" (N 2.5.1).

EXPERIENCE AND REALITY

A second major truth of the dark night that is illustrated by the image of the burning log is that there is a difference between reality and our interpretation of reality. "This divine purge stirs up all the foul and vicious humors of which the soul was never before aware; never did it realize there was so much evil in itself. . . . Now they are brought to light and seen clearly. Although the soul is no worse than before . . . it feels clearly that it is so bad as to be not only unworthy that God see it but deserving of his abhorrence" (N 2.10.2).

In the dark night, when the light of contemplation shines most brightly, everything that was once hidden is "brought to light and seen clearly" (N 2.10.2). Or as the psalmist writes, "You have set our iniquities before you, our secret sins in the light of your countenance" (Ps 90:8). In the dark night, we do not see the countenance of God but rather our sinful self reflected in God's face. In consequence, John tells us that the soul "feels clearly [parécele claro] that it is so bad as to be not only unworthy that God see it but deserving of his abhorrence" (N 2.10.2). This is another example of how we misjudge our spiritual condition from an emotional perspective.

Parécele means "to seem" or "to form a judgment." Because we feel unworthy of God, we make the erroneous judgment that God abhors us.

As grace purges us, we feel that we are becoming worse. "Everything seems to be functioning in reverse" (N 1.8.3). However, the opposite is true. We are not regressing but progressing. Awareness of our sinfulness is an important step on the road to transformation. However, we do not recognize this truth because we tend to judge ourselves from an emotional perspective rather than from a spiritual standpoint. When the light of contemplation shines most brightly within us, all we see is our own darkness and, like the psalmist, we cry out, "Turn your gaze away from me, that I may smile again" (Ps 39:13). God averts his gaze, so to speak, when the light of contemplation shines *less* brightly. "But sometimes the contemplation shines less forcibly so they may have the opportunity to observe and even rejoice over the work being achieved, for then these good effects are revealed. It is as though one were to stop work and take the iron out of the forge to observe what is being accomplished. Thus the soul is able to perceive the good it was unaware of while the work was proceeding. So too, when the flame stops acting upon the wood, there is a chance to see how much the wood has been enkindled by it" (N 2.10.6).

When the light of contemplation shines less brightly upon the inner recesses of our souls, we feel relief and joy because we are released from being absorbed in our inner darkness. At such moments, we are able to see and rejoice in the work that contemplation is accomplishing within us.

UNION

"The eternal pearl received us into itself as water receives a ray
of light and yet remains unsundered and serene."[3] This passage
from Dante's *Paradiso* is a symbol of a person in union with
God. It conveys that, in union, God and the soul are both two
and one; they are distinct yet interpenetrate one another. Just
as every molecule of water is completely permeated and utterly
saturated with light, yet is distinct from the light, so too is
a person in union completely united with yet distinct from
God. John symbolizes this reality as a log that is so permeated
by fire that it has become a glowing ember—"the fire transforms the wood into itself" (N 2.10.1).

This simultaneous oneness and twoness asserts that, in
union, our will is in complete conformity with God's will,
without our individuality being surrendered. Though "all the
acts of the soul . . . stem from God" (F 1.4), the soul retains
its freedom as it gives its consent to God's grace. This paradox
is best expressed by St. Paul's words, "The life I live now is not
my own; Christ is living within me, yet I still live my human
life, but it is a life of faith in the Son of God" (Gal 2:20).

A person in union with God becomes a sacrament of the
divine. Transformed by grace, he or she becomes a transforming presence to others. Or as John writes, "Once transformed,
the wood . . . possesses the properties and performs the
actions of the fire . . . It is hot and it gives off heat; it is brilliant and it illumines" (N 2.10.1).

Quoting the sixth-century theologian Pseudo-Dionysius,
St. Thomas Aquinas writes that the "the good is diffusive
of itself." To illustrate this truth, Dionysius compares God's
goodness to the sun, a largesse universal that cannot help but
spread its warmth and light to all beings.[4] Similarly, a soul

transformed into God "is hot and it gives off heat; it is brilliant and it illumines" (N 2.10.1).

What this means is that people who are in the state of union share the nature of God by grace; they possess the power to enkindle and awaken the love of God in others. St. Teresa, writing to her sisters, says, "This fire of love in you enkindles their souls and with every other virtue you will be always awakening them. Such service will not be small but very great and very pleasing to the Lord" (IC 7.4.14). Can there be a life that is more generative?

DARK NIGHT AS PURGATORY

> [From our image of the burning log] we can infer the manner in which souls suffer in purgatory. . . . These imperfections are the fuel that catches on fire, and once they are gone there is nothing left to burn. So it is here on earth; when the imperfections are gone, the soul's suffering terminates, and joy remains. (N 2.10.5)

This statement contains an important truth regarding the nature of purgatory, namely, that purgatory is not an arbitrary punishment imposed from without, like a judge passing down a sentence upon a criminal. It is a process that lasts as long as is needed for a person to be purified. This truth is symbolized in Dante's *Purgatorio.*

As Dante and Virgil climb the Mount of Purgation, they hear souls shouting in one voice, "Glory to God in the Highest!" This happens each time a soul has been purified and ascends from purgatory to heaven. For Dante, a soul leaves purgatory when it experiences that it has been completely purified by God's grace. "The will attests to its own purgation"

(*Purgatorio* 21.61). Charles Williams says that this is Dante's theory of divine satisfaction: "God is satisfied when we are satisfied."[5] "Imperfections are the fuel that catches on fire, and once they are gone there is nothing left to burn. . . . When the imperfections are gone, the soul's suffering terminates, and joy remains" (N 2.10.5).

For Reflection

On Christmas day, 1886, St. Thérèse said she received the greatest grace of her life: "the grace of leaving childhood" (S 98), along with the grace to control her "extreme touchiness" (S 97). It all began after the family had returned home from attending midnight Mass. As Thérèse was climbing the stairs to go to bed, by chance, she overheard a remark made by her father Louis to her sister Céline. It was the French custom to fill the shoes of the family's youngest child with little gifts; since Thérèse was no longer a child but a teenager, this custom was age inappropriate. As Louis noticed Thérèse's shoes in front of the fireplace he groaned, "Thérèse ought to have outgrown all this sort of thing, and I hope this will be the last time."[6]

"Those words pierced my heart" (S 98), said Thérèse. However, it actually turned out for the best because her father's words were the instrument by which Thérèse realized she had never grown up. "I was still in the *swaddling clothes of a child!*" (S 97). Her father's

CONTINUED

remark pierced through Thérèse's "habitual ign... (N 2.5.1) regarding her lack of emotional maturity. ... was a turning point in her life, and it all began when ... overheard a remark made by her father.

Just like God brought Augustine "to a realization of [his] miserable state" as he passed through a certain district in Milan and saw a drunken beggar, so too, God awakened Thérèse to her emotional immaturity as she overheard her father's remark while she was going up to her room.

Sometimes we see something, hear something, or read something that changes the course of our life.

Have you ever considered that these "chance" events are actually the context in which God's grace entered your life?

Fired with Love's Urgent Longings

A FORETASTE OF GOD

John writes of two enkindlings of our desire for God. The first is the result of consolation given to beginners, which starts to detach them from the things of this world and helps them find their joy in the things of God. "The soul finds its joy in spending lengthy periods at prayer, perhaps even entire nights; its penances are pleasures; its fasts happiness and the sacraments and spiritual conversations are its consolations" (N 1.1.3). This joy, though it has its origin in God, is more sensual than spiritual. It moves the emotions but has little effect upon the will.

The second enkindling is the result of God's presence as contemplation, which engenders a deep spiritual love in the will, which is qualitatively different from the love that is imparted by consolation. "Although this enkindling of love . . . is in some way similar to what occurs in the sensory part of the soul, it is as different from it . . . as is the soul from the body or the spiritual part from the sensory part. For this enkindling of love occurs in the spirit. . . . [The soul is] wounded by a strong divine love, and it has a certain feeling and foretaste of God" (N 2.11.1).

This foretaste is an experience of God that wounds us with a poignant desire for God, whom we cannot fully "possess" (N 2.11.5) in this life. We feel stranded between two worlds, one dying, the other powerless to be born. We "find rest in nothing" (N 2.11.6). As John expresses it in his poem "Stanzas of the Soul that Suffers with Longing to See God": "I die because I do not die."

"Why does God make us wait so long?" asks St. Augustine. He answers, "God stretches our desire through delay, stretches our soul through desire, and makes it large by stretching."[1] We know that this longing has its origin in God because it dilates the soul and gives it the capacity to be connected to the world by love. In contrast, there are longings that shrink the soul and isolate it from the world. We have an example of this in Alfred Lord Tennyson's poem "Mariana" in which a woman is pining away with desire as she awaits her lover's return. Nothing in the world matters to her except her lover.

> "My life is dreary,
> He cometh not," she said;
> She said, "I am aweary, aweary,
> I would that I were dead!" . . .
>
> "The night is dreary,
> He cometh not," she said;
> She said, "I am aweary, aweary,
> I would that I were dead!" . . .
>
> "The day is dreary,
> He cometh not," she said;
> She said, "I am aweary, aweary,
> I would that I were dead!" . . .

"My life is dreary,
He cometh not," she said;
She said, "I am aweary, aweary,
I would that I were dead!"[2]

In two ways, Mariana resembles the person whom John describes in this chapter. Both are wounded by love, and both have lost interest in the things of this world. However, there is a major difference between the two. Mariana's longing is a moping affectation that isolates her from life, whereas the person wounded by God not only has been detached from his or her inordinate desires for the things of this world but also has been given the capacity to be connected to the world by love.

For Reflection

Detachment is the fruit of God's grace operating in our lives. The more we are "wounded by a strong divine love" (N 2.11.1), the more our desire for the things of this world decreases.

Have you ever noticed that as your longing for God increases, the things of this world have less of a hold upon you?

NIGHT 2.12–14

The Imparting of Wisdom and Love

‿‿‿

God "teaches without the noise of words," writes St.
Thérèse. "Never have I heard Him speak, but I feel that
He is within me at each moment . . . guiding and inspiring
me with what I must say and do" (S 179). We find an example
of this instinctive knowledge of God's guidance operating in
Thérèse's life in the following event.

One day when St. Thérèse lay dying, her prioress,
Mother Gonzague, came into the infirmary and noticed
that someone had left both the door and the window
open, which created a strong draft. She became angry and
insisted that Thérèse tell her who was responsible. Thérèse
told Mother Gonzague that the culprit was Sister St. Stan-
islaus. However, as she was doing so, the following happened inside of Thérèse. "I told Mother Prioress the truth,
but while I was speaking, there came to my mind a more
charitable way of expressing it than the one I was going
to use. . . . I followed my inspiration, and God rewarded
me with a great interior peace" (LC 138). This is an example of how "God teaches the soul secretly and instructs it in
the perfection of love without its doing anything or understanding how this happens" (N 2.5.1).

Thérèse was highly attuned to hearing God's voice because of her charity, which inclined her will to attend to God. As St. Thomas Aquinas teaches, divine wisdom "comes from charity" (*Summa Theologiae* [ST] II, II, q. 45, a. 4), which creates an "instinctive affinity" (ST II, II, q. 45, a. 2) between God and the soul.[1] According to Josef Pieper, this "instinctive affinity" is "an inner attunement, thanks to the unerring instincts of the lover."[2] In other words, the depth of our love determines the degree of our inner attunement to God's voice. This is why John teaches that "God never bestows [*nunca da*] mystical wisdom without love, since love itself infuses it" (N 2.12.2).

God *nunca da*, that is, *never gives* wisdom without imparting to the will the inclination to love. However, we can resist this inclination. Often we do so because love threatens our complacency, disrupts our routines, and intrudes upon our plans. Is it any wonder that we "do not want to enter the dark night or allow [ourselves] to be placed in it" (A Prol 3)? Only love can teach us the paradox of the Gospel. We possess only what we are willing to give away; we can find ourselves only by losing ourselves.

THE MINISTRY OF ANGELS

John teaches that God tempers or provides "certain modification[s]" (N 2.12.3) of the divine inflow through the ministry of angels.[3] God adjusts the amount of contemplation we receive according to our capacity, for "whatever is received is received according to the mode of the receiver" (N 2.16.4).

> This contemplation infuses both love and wisdom in each soul according to its capacity and necessity. . . . This wisdom descends from God through the first hierarchies [of

angels] unto the last, and from these last to humans. For ordinarily these works and inspirations are derived from God by means of the angels, and the angels also in turn give them one to another without delay. This communication is like that of a ray of sunlight shining through many windows placed one after the other. Although it is true that of itself the ray of light passes through them all, nevertheless each window communicates this light to the other with a certain modification. . . . Humans, the last to whom this loving contemplation of God is communicated . . . must receive it according to their own mode, in a very limited and painful way. (N 2.12.2–3)

We have to grow in our capacity to look upon God before we endeavor to do so; otherwise, we will be annihilated. As Scripture attests, no one can see the face of God and live (Ex 33:20). We have a symbol of this reality in Dante's *Paradiso*. As Beatrice, who is a sacrament of God, guides Dante upward into the presence of God, her face grows more luminous. Her eyes, her smile, and her whole countenance grow brighter in proportion to the depths of the divine truths that she imparts to Dante. However, Beatrice restrains the outward expression of her radiance, lest it overwhelm Dante's capacity to receive it. At one point, as Dante peers into Beatrice's eyes, she tells him, "Were I to smile . . . you would be turned into ash."[4] It is only after Dante's capacity to receive divine truth and love has expanded that Beatrice says to him, "Open your eyes and turn them full on me! / You have seen things whose power has made you able / to bear the bright smile of my ecstasy!"[5] It was because of Beatrice's love for Dante that she shielded him from God's presence as she communicated God to him. How much she revealed to

Dante depended upon his capacity to receive. There is much to ponder here. Just as God does not reveal to us more than we can bear, so too should we deal with one another.

The virtue of honesty is never harsh or insulting; rather, it is a part of temperance and "a kind of spiritual beauty" (ST II, II, q. 145, a. 4), writes St. Thomas Aquinas. Honesty does not wield truth as a weapon but "speaks the truth in love" (Eph 4:15). Tempering truth according to the capacity of the receiver neither dilutes the truth nor sidesteps an issue. It is sharing in the ministry of God's angels who make "certain modification[s]" (N 2.12.3) as they impart truth according to the dictates of love.

LOVE BOTH ENGENDERS AND CASTS OUT FEAR

In the dark night, grace can inflame "the soul . . . with a singular boldness [that makes it] do strange [*extrañas e inusitadas*] things" (N 2.13.5). *Extrañas e inusitadas*, which translated literally means "strange and unusual," may best be interpreted within the context of this passage to mean "unaccustomed, unused to, or unfamiliar." It refers to the fortitude to do God's will in the face of our fears, to do things that we feel unfit and ill equipped to perform. It pertains to the courage to do God's will at the expense of stepping outside our character or putting ourselves in a situation where we feel either anxious or extremely ill at ease. It means to venture beyond the boundaries of our most deeply ingrained personality traits for the love of God. Such is the "courage of love" (N 2.13.6).

We have an example of such courage in the life of Nathaniel Hawthorne. In 1856, when Hawthorne was the American consul to England, he visited an almshouse in Liverpool. He recounts the event in *The English Notebooks*.

After this, we went to the ward where the children were kept, and, on entering this, we saw, in the first place, two or three unlovely and unwholesome little imps, who were lazily playing together. One of them (a child about six years old, but I know not whether girl or boy) immediately took the strangest fancy for me. It was a wretched, pale, half-torpid little thing, with a humor in its eyes which the Governor said was the scurvy. I never saw, till a few moments afterwards, a child that I should feel less inclined to fondle. But this little, sickly, humor-eaten fright prowled around me, taking hold of my skirts, following at my heels, and at last held up its hands, smiled in my face, and, standing directly before me, insisted on my taking it up! Not that it said a word, for I rather think it was underwitted, and could not talk; but its face expressed such perfect confidence that it was going to be taken up and made much of, that it was impossible not to do it. It was as if God had promised the child this favor on my behalf, and that I must needs fulfill the contract. I held my undesirable burden a little while; and, after setting the child down, it still followed me, holding two of my fingers and playing with them, just as if it were a child of my own. It was a foundling, and out of all human kind it chose me to be its father! We went up stairs into another ward; and, on coming down again, there was this same child waiting for me, with a sickly smile round its defaced mouth, and in its dim red eyes. . . . I wish I had not touched the imp; and yet I never should have forgiven myself if I had repelled its advances.[6]

Hawthorne's choice to pick up this poor child was excruciatingly painful, more than anyone could have ever imagined, for he was extremely introverted and almost pathologically shy;

he had a deep revulsion for anything ugly and was violently repulsed by anything deformed.

Eight years later and seven months before his death, he lifted the veil on how costly and transformative his choice really had been. In his last published work, *Our Old Home: A Series of English Sketches,* he writes of this event. However, Hawthorne deliberately concealed his identity, for he writes of the incident as if he were an outside observer.

> By-and-by we came to the ward where the children were kept. . . . Among the children was a wretched, pale half-torpid little thing . . . with a humor in its eyes and face, which the governor said was scurvy. . . . It prowled about [an Englishman of our company] like a pet kitten, rubbing against his legs, following everywhere at his heals, pulling at his coattails, and, at last, exerting all the speed that its poor limbs were capable of, got directly before him and held forth its arms, mutely insisting on being taken up. . . . It was as if God had promised the poor child this favor on his behalf . . . and he was bound to fulfill the contract. Nevertheless, it could be no easy thing for him to do, he being a person burthened with more than an Englishman's customary reserve, shy of actual contact with human beings, afflicted with a peculiar distaste for whatever was ugly, and, furthermore, accustomed to that habit of observation from an insulated stand-point which is said (but, I hope erroneously) to have the tendency of putting ice into the blood.
>
> *So I watched the struggle in his mind with a good deal of interest, and am seriously of the opinion that he did an heroic act, and effected more than he dreamed of towards his final salvation, when he took up the loathsome child and caressed it as tenderly as if he had been its father.*[7] (italics added)

This was a critical turning point in Hawthorne's spiritual life, a deliberate choice that impacted him more than he realized at the time the choice was made, and a crucial step "towards his final salvation." What is important to note is that Hawthorne's choice to pick up the child was an act of "singular boldness," indeed a "strange thing" (N 2.13.6) that was invisible to the eye. Such is the "courage of love" (N 2.13.6).

I WENT OUT UNSEEN

What gives us the courage to do "strange" things? In a word, grace. In chapter 14, John focuses upon a specific form of grace, the grace that calms our fears and reduces the strength of our "passions and appetites." This grace enables us to step outside the familiar, to leave our "house" (N 2.14.1). It is important to note that before perfect union with God is achieved, grace does not eliminate our fears and appetites; they are only "stilled" and "quelled" (N 14.1), or to use John's image, "all the members of [our] house are asleep" (N 2.14.1). When our fears and appetites are quelled, like Hawthorne, we are given the capacity to love in ways that we never were able to do before. Then we can stand in amazement of God's grace that is able to accomplish within us "more than all we can ask or imagine" (Eph 3:20).

For Reflection

Can you remember a time when God's grace imparted to you a "singular boldness" (N 2.13.5) that gave you the strength to act with the "courage of love"

CONTINUED

(N 2.13.6)? What have you found that helps you to dispose yourself to receive this courage?

St. Francis de Sales admonishes us to "act on the minds of others . . . as the angels do, graciously and without coercion."[8]

Where in your conversations are God's angels inviting you to make "certain modification[s]" (N 2.12.3) according to the dictates of love?

The Deepening of Transformation

In darkness, and secure,
by the secret ladder, disguised,
—ah, the sheer grace!—
in darkness and concealment,
my house being now all stilled. (*Dark Night*, stanza 2)

From chapter 15 through chapter 24, John comments upon the second stanza of his poem. Chapter 15 consists of only one paragraph. Its main purpose is to prevent a misunderstanding, namely, that even though John will be commenting upon a new stanza, he will not be dealing with different material; rather, his commentary on stanza 2 will be a continuation of what he has already said in his explication of stanza 1. "The soul in its song continues to recount some of the properties of the darkness of this night and mentions again the happiness resulting from them" (N 2.15.1).

Keeping this perspective in mind will prevent some unnecessary confusion, for readers are likely to ask, "How is what John is saying in these chapters any different from what he has already said?" There is a difference, but the difference is in degree not in kind. The following chapters are a continuation of what has already been stated. This chapter reminds us of the seamless unity of the *one* dark night.

NIGHT 2.16

Walking Securely

[The dark night] deprives [the soul] of the ability to find pleasure in anything. It binds the imagination and impedes it from doing any good discursive work. It makes the memory cease, the intellect becomes dark and unable to understand anything, and hence it causes the will also to become arid and constrained, and all the faculties empty and useless. (N 2.16.1)

The above passage refers to the psychological and spiritual effects of the night of the spirit. The following passage lists these effects that a person experiences at the time he or she enters the night of sense, the transition from meditation to contemplation (N 1.9). "[God] binds the interior faculties and leaves no support in the intellect, nor satisfaction in the will, nor remembrance in the memory. . . . [There] is a powerlessness . . . to meditate and make use of the imagination" (N 1.9.7–8).

The similarity between the effects that we experience in the night of sense and the night of the spirit are rooted in the unity of the one dark night. Let us look at one example of this unity by making some parallels between a person entering the night of sense and a person submerged in the night of the spirit.

SIMILAR EFFECTS OF THE NIGHT OF SENSE AND THE NIGHT OF THE SPIRIT

There are three major effects of contemplation (the inflow of God into the soul) that are common to both nights. The first is that the appetites are put to sleep. Second, the imagination is bound, which impedes us from meditating discursively. This in turn causes the third effect, namely, the will becomes arid and we feel we are powerless (see N 1.9, N 1.10, and N 2.16.2).

SIMILAR REACTIONS

These effects cause a similar reaction in both nights: fear. When we enter the night of sense and are unable to find joy in the things of God, we are afraid that we are "not serving God but turning back" (N 1.9.3). Similarly, in the night of the spirit, we are afraid that we are separated from God by "a dense and burdensome cloud" (N 2.16.1).

SIMILAR ADVICE

In order to calm our fears, the advice that John gives us when we are in either of the nights is the same: consider the spiritual fruits, not the psychological effects.

In the night of sense, John counsels us to become aware of the fact that our desire for God is being enkindled (N 1.11.1); that we are growing in self-knowledge and humility (N 1.12.2); and that we are becoming less judgmental toward our neighbor (N 1.12.8). Similarly, in the night of the spirit, when we feel arid and void of desire for all things, John assures us that we "walk securely" because "the soul's evils are impeded [*impedida*]" (N 2.16.3).

Notice the juxtaposition of images in John's statement. We walk securely when we are impeded. *Impedida,* derived from the Latin *impedire,* means "to shackle the feet." In short, we walk securely when our feet are shackled.

Let us try to understand John's imagery by means of a question. When you feel that your "memory cease[s]" to function, your "intellect become[s] dark," and you are "unable to understand anything," and "over all this hangs a dense and burdensome cloud that afflicts [your] soul" (N 2.16.1), have you also noticed that your inordinate desires are "shackled"?

This is why we walk securely. We are protected from ourselves. "[A] soul never strays except through its appetites [which in the dark night] are impeded. . . . [Such souls] are not only liberated from themselves, . . . [but also liberated from] the world and the devil" (N 2.16.2).

In consequence, John advises us to become aware of everything that we are experiencing, not only the emotional effect of the dark night but also the spiritual consequence. "[Try to] observe closely at the time of these darknesses [and you] will see clearly how little [your] appetites and faculties are distracted with useless and harmful things and how secure [you] are from vainglory, from pride and presumption, from an empty and false joy, and from other evils. By walking in darkness [you] not only avoid going astray but advance rapidly, because [you] gain the virtues" (N 2.16.3).

The end of this passage adds a paradoxical dimension to John's image of being shackled. Not only do we advance securely, but also we proceed rapidly. The implication is that when we feel that the whole of our spiritual quest is empty and void; when we have lost the motive of action; and when prayer, works of charity, and ministry seem meaningless, we advance rapidly in virtue, and a great transformation is being accomplished, if we choose to continue to put one wearied foot in front of the another. As we have seen, John places before us the fact that our interpretation of our experience is often at odds with reality. We feel we are wandering aimlessly in a desert, as we progress toward the Promised Land. We think we are "getting lost rather than marching on successfully and profitably" (N 2.16.8). We feel we have lost sight of God when we are "engulf[ed] in the dark night" (N 2.16.10), but we do not realize that the dark night actually is the presence of God within us. We feel that God is absent because God is intimately present. From an emotional perspective, it is the worst of times, but from a spiritual perspective, it is the best of times. As C. S. Lewis writes in *The Screwtape Letters*, "Do not be deceived, Wormwood. Our cause is never more in danger than when a human, no longer desiring, but still intending, to do our Enemy's [God's] will, looks around upon a universe from which every trace of Him seems to have vanished, and asks why he has been forsaken, and still obeys."[1]

When we feel that our mind and emotions are devoid of God, we know that God is nourishing our will, when we continue to put one wearied, shackled foot in front of the another.

THE ROAD OF SUFFERING

We walk securely in the dark night because the Guide who leads us is wise and loving. He protects us from ourselves by shackling our inordinate appetites as he guides us along the road of suffering.

> There is another reason the soul walks securely in these darknesses: It advances by suffering. Suffering is a surer and even more advantageous road than that of joy and action

[*gozar y hacer*]. First, in suffering, strength is given to the soul by God. In its doing and enjoying, the soul exercises its own weakness and imperfections. Second, in suffering, virtues are practiced and acquired, and the soul is purified and made wiser and more cautious.

Another more basic reason the soul walks securely in darkness is that this light, or obscure wisdom, so absorbs and engulfs the soul in the dark night of contemplation and brings it so near God that it is protected and freed from all that is not God. Since the soul, as it were, is undergoing a cure to regain its health, which is God himself, His Majesty restricts it to a diet, to abstinence from all things, and causes it to lose its appetite for them all. This effect resembles the cure of sick people when esteemed by members of their household: They are kept inside so that neither air nor light may harm them; others try not to disturb them by the noise of their footsteps or even whisperings, and give them a very delicate and limited amount of food, substantial rather than tasty. (N 2.16.9–10)

To understand what John means by the road of suffering, we need to contrast it with the road of "joy and action [*gozar y hacer*]," which is the road of good works. *Gozar* means "to enjoy" or "to find fruition," whereas *hacer* means "to make" or "to produce." Although there is nothing wrong with finding joy in good works, there is a danger in our performance of them. For on this road "the soul exercises [*ejercita*] its own weakness and imperfections" (N 2.16.9). *Ejercita* means "to put into practice."

In book three of *The Ascent of Mount Carmel*, John tells us the spiritual dangers that attend the practice of good works. He says that the "exercise [*ejercicio*] of any of the virtues [or] the practice [*ejercicio*] of the works of mercy" (A 3.27.1) are susceptible to "vanity, pride, vainglory and presumption" (A 3.28.2). The reason we often fall prey to these harms is because we are "unable to rejoice [*gozarse*] over [our] works without esteeming [*estimarlas*] them" (A 3.28.2). *Estimarlas* means "to value," "to esteem," or "to make much of." Thus, we do not walk securely on the "road . . . of joy and action" (N 2.16.9) because we are susceptible to pride and investing our self-worth in the work of our hands.

Another reason we do not walk securely on this road is "since [we] look for satisfaction in [our] works, [we] usually do not perform them unless [we] see that some gratification or praise will result from them" (A 3.28.4). Therefore, we can be tempted to devote ourselves tirelessly to a charitable project that we find exciting or rewarding, while neglecting the lackluster duties of our vocation in life. We see a tragic-comic example of this in Charles Dickens's character Mrs. Jellyby. By means of her "telescopic philanthropy,"[2] she dedicates every waking hour to helping "the natives of Borrio-boola-Gha, on the left bank of the Niger"[3] grow coffee, while neglecting the needs of her children and husband. Mrs. Jellyby may have profited greatly had she reflected upon John's precaution.

> It should be noted that among the many wiles of the devil for deceiving spiritual persons, the most common is deceiv-ing them under the appearance of good rather than of evil, for the devil already knows that they will scarcely choose a recognized evil. Thus you should always be suspicious of what appears good, especially when not obliged by obedi-ence. To do the right thing, and be safe in such a matter, you ought to take the proper counsel.

Let, then, the first precaution be that, without the command of obedience, you never take upon yourself any work: apart from the obligations of your state—however good and full of charity it may seem, whether for yourself or for anyone else inside or outside the house. By such a practice you will win merit and security, avoid possession, and flee from harm and evils unknown to you. (Pre 10–11)

"The command of obedience" consists in attending to "the obligations of [one's] state" in life (Pre 11)—in a word, doing one's duty. Walking the path of duty involves a twofold suffering, as was indicated in our earlier example of Ann. By dedicating herself to raising her children, Ann let go of her dream of being a full professor of English literature and embraced the burden of a thousand and one thankless tasks of being a stay-at-home mom. Ann's choice is at the heart of the dark night. As John writes, "As regards this road to union, entering on the road means leaving one's own road" (A 2.4.5). Leaving one's own road is a good metaphor for the type of suffering that John focuses upon in the passive night of the spirit.

Passive (*pasiva*) and passion (*pasión*) are derived from the same Latin root word *pati*, which means "to suffer," "to undergo," or "to submit" to what is imposed from an external agent. In short, God chooses what we will do. This is why we walk securely on the road of suffering. Conversely, the danger that lies on the road of joy and action is that we will choose the good works we perform. Thus, our choices may be determined more by our ego and self-satisfaction than by God.

A DEEP AND DELICATE LISTENING

> A question immediately arises here: Since the things of God in themselves produce good in the soul, are beneficial, and give assurance, why does God in this night darken the appetites and faculties so that these derive no satisfaction in such good things and find it difficult to be occupied with them? (N 2.16.4)

The answer may be stated as follows: God deprives us of a good in order that we may grow in the capacity to receive a greater good. God weans us away from the goods of this world by means of the "good milk and tender food" (N 1.1.2) of consolation. Then, God "wean[s] [us] from the . . . sweet food of [consolation]" (N 1.12.1) by bringing us into the night of sense. Once purged from our inordinate desire for consolation, we can then experience "the sweet idleness of the contemplation that is being communicated to [us]" (N 1.11.4).

In this chapter, John teaches that in the night of the spirit, we must undergo a deeper and more spiritual purification than was suffered in the night of sense. In the night of sense, we have to become detached from our desire for consolation and learn to "be content simply with a loving and peaceful attentiveness to God [contemplation]" (N 1.10.4). In the night of the spirit, God detaches us even from our desire to experience the loving and peaceful presence of contemplation. We must learn to sit in a spiritual void as God draws us "more deeply into [our] inner depths" (N 2.23.4), where we "become established in quietude and solitary love" (C 35.1). "When . . . souls are conscious . . . of being placed in [this] solitude . . . they should even forget the practice of loving attentiveness" (F 3.35); this practice "would impede and disquiet them and make noise in the profound silence of their senses and their spirit, which they possess for the sake of this deep and delicate listening" (F 3.34).

What diminishes our capacity for a deep and delicate listening is the psychic noise that our inordinate desires create. What blocks out the profound silence of God that dwells in the center of our hearts is the deafening tumult of our will. This is symbolized in Ray Bradbury's novel *The Martian Chronicles*, where earthlings, in their frenzy to colonize Mars, are unable to be present to the deep silence that surrounds them.

> The rockets came like drums, beating in the night . . . like locusts, swarming and settling in blooms of rosy smoke. And from the rockets ran men with hammers in their hands to beat the strange world into a shape that was familiar to the eye, to bludgeon away all the strangeness, their mouths fringed with nails so they resembled steel-toothed carnivores, spitting them into their swift hands as they hammered up frame cottages and scuttled over roofs with shingles to blot out the eerie stars, and fit green shades to pull against the night. And when the carpenters had hurried on, the women came in with flowerpots and chintz and pans and set up a kitchen clamor to cover the silence that Mars made waiting outside the door and the shaded window.[4]

So too the silence of God is covered over by the clamor of our will. In the innermost dwelling place of our heart, God patiently waits for us to enter that sacred space of inner silence. There, God speaks. "The Father spoke one Word, which was His Son, and this Word he speaks always in eternal silence, and in silence must it be heard by the soul" (SLL 100).

For Reflection

When you feel that "over [you] hangs a dense and burdensome cloud that afflicts [your] soul," have you ever been conscious of the fact that God's grace is simultaneously protecting you from "harmful things" (N 2.16.1), namely, that he is shackling your inordinate appetites? If you "observe closely" (N 2.16.3) that God is protecting you in this regard, you will experience God's presence in your soul. Are you able to discern the spiritual fruits of the dark night in the midst of its emotional effects?

Pope Emeritus Benedict XVI said the following in a homily on the importance of silence in the spiritual life. "Unbeknown to them, people are increasingly becoming immersed in a virtual dimension because of the audio-visual messages that accompany their life from morning to night. It has reached such a level as to give rise to talk about an anthropological mutation, [the inability] of remaining for long periods in silence and solitude."[5]

We live in a noisy world. All day long, our over-stimulated culture bombards us with a barrage of information, through newspapers, billboards, radio, television, Internet, and so forth. We have lost the predictability for privacy; cell phones, text messages, and e-mail have made us completely accessible to others, and everyone expects an instant reply.

CONTINUED

As a result of being both a victim and a participant of our noisy world, all of us are in danger of the anthropological mutation that Pope Benedict speaks of, namely, the eroding of our capacity to sit in silence. The more this happens, the more our ability to sit quietly in the presence of God diminishes.

Although we cannot change the noisy world around us, there are many lifestyle choices that we can make that will decrease the amount of physical and psychic noise to which we are exposed. Literally and figuratively we can turn down the volume in our lives. John tells us that "it is great wisdom to know how to be silent" (SLL 109). This wisdom is a gift from God. Ask God what you should do in order to incorporate silence into your life.

Secret Wisdom

~⚬~

In darkness and secure,

By the secret ladder, disguised. (*Dark Night*, stanza 2)

In the above verse, John introduces three terms (secret, ladder, and disguised) that he will develop in the next few chapters. The first two terms, secret and ladder, are passive in nature, that is, they refer to what God accomplishes within us; the third term, "disguised," refers to "the way [the soul] conducts itself in this night" (N 2.17.1). Let us examine these terms more closely.

SECRET

There are two reasons the wisdom that "dark contemplation" imparts is "secret." The first is that its origin cannot be comprehended, for it arises out of the depths of the soul. It is the result of neither reasoning nor thinking; it is "not acquired" but "infuse[d]." In consequence, "the soul neither knows nor understands how this [wisdom] comes to pass" (N 2.17.2). We simply become aware that it has entered our conscious mind. We find an example of this in C. S. Lewis's account of the moment of his conversion to Christianity.

"When we set out [for the zoo] I did not believe that Jesus Christ is the Son of God, and when we reached the zoo I did. Yet I had not exactly spent the journey in thought. Nor in a great emotion. . . . It was more like when a man, after long sleep, still lying motionless in bed, becomes aware that he is now awake."[1]

Lewis simply became aware that he believed. How he became aware was "secret" to him. He could give no explanation; it just happened. Likewise, all of us can attest to such experiences of God's "secret" wisdom. For example, how often in the midst of a conversation have you known instinctively what to say or not to say? You didn't know *how* you knew; you became aware *that* you knew.

The second reason this wisdom is secret is that it is "ineffable"; it cannot be expressed, not only when the soul is being purified "but also afterward in the illumination." In short, we cannot put into words the "the effects it produces" (N 2.17.3) in us. It is incommunicable because it is incomparable. It cannot be compared to any experience or expressed by any idea or image. We are at a loss to say, "It is like this or that." Our mind "cannot form an idea or picture of it in order to speak of it" (N 2.17.3). This is true because ideas and images have their origins in sense experience, whereas God's "secret" wisdom is not communicated through the senses but is directly infused in the soul. In consequence, there is no perceptible, and therefore communicable, impression imprinted upon memory. "The traces . . . God leaves in [us] are unrecognizable" because they "are the footsteps of one walking on water imperceptible" (N 2.17.8). However, something is perceived, though it cannot be expressed, the deep emotional impress of God's wisdom imprinted in the depths of our souls.

Dante attempted to express this reality by a similar image. In the last canto of the *Paradiso*, he has an experience of God, which leaves a deep impression upon his soul but not the ability to express it.

> As one sees in dreams and wakes to find
> the emotional impression of his vision
> still powerful while its parts fade from his mind
> just such am I, having lost nearly all
> the vision itself, while in my heart I feel
> the sweetness of it yet distill and fall.
> So, in the sun, the footprints fade from snow.[2]

The depth and sweetness of God's wisdom distilled in the soul is of such an intimate nature that we are both unable and "unwilling" (N 2.17.3) to express it. "Contemplation is indescribable" (N 2.17.5), and there is a "great repugnance in speaking about it" (N 2.17.5). This is because the wisdom is "so sublime an understanding and delicate a spiritual feeling" (N 2.17.3) that any attempt to clothe it in conceptual thought or express it in words would do it violence. "The language of God . . . silences [our] entire ability" (N 2.17.3) to adequately express God's wisdom in human speech. The best we can hope to accomplish is to "let something of [our] experiences [of grace] overflow in figures, comparisons and similitudes" (C Prol 1). However, the *something* that can be expressed is elusive because of the "ineffability of divine language" (N 2.17.4).

INNER SOLITUDE

Amma Syncletica said, "It is possible to be solitary in one's mind while living in a crowd, and it is possible for one who is solitary to live in the crowd of his own thoughts."[3] Being solitary in one's mind is what John calls "inner solitude" (Co 9). It is a secret interior dwelling place where the maddening crowd of our thoughts and inordinate appetites are hushed. To arrive at this place is the work of contemplation. The soul is "brought into a place far removed from every creature" and feels it has "been led into a remarkable deep and vast wilderness . . . into an immense unbounded desert . . . vaster and more solitary" (N 2.17.6) than anything it has ever experienced.

In this process of transformation, the grace of being brought into this vast solitude is given to us "occasionally" (N 2.17.6). Gradually, this inner solitude becomes a state of being in the soul. The Bride "has become [so] established in the quietude of solitary love [that] she is settled in God and God in her" (C 35.1) for "in solitude [she] has built a nest" (C 35.3).

For Reflection

Can you remember a time when you instinctively knew what God was asking you to do, without either "know[ing] [or] understand[ing] how this [came] to pass" (N 2.17.2)?

If you have had this experience, then you know what it means when John says that God "infuses" wisdom, which is different from knowledge that has been "acquired" (N 2.17.2).

NIGHT 2.18

The Secret Ladder

~~⌇~~

John explains the first reason that "secret wisdom is . . . a ladder" (N 2.18.1) by means of an image. Just as a soldier "ascends a ladder to pillage . . . fortresses containing goods and treasures," so too "by this secret contemplation, the soul ascends in order to plunder, know, and possess the goods and treasures of heaven." It ascends "from virtue to virtue (as from step to step)" until it obtains "the treasure of the fortress— beatitude" (N 2.18.1).

Underlying this image is a Scholastic principle regarding the relationship between grace and growth in virtue, namely, that "all means must be proportionate to their end" (A 2.8.2). Since "beatitude" (union with God) is the end of virtue, then God's grace must be the means to this end. "By this secret contemplation, the soul ascends," that is, grace is the means by which we practice and grow in the virtues (N 2.18.1). This fact is hidden from our conscious mind because in the moment of choice we are so absorbed in the effort that we are exerting in practicing virtue that we are unaware of the "secret contemplation" that gives us the strength to make the effort. The virtues grow, but "the soul neither knows nor understands how this comes to pass" (N 2.17.2).

To Humble Is to Exalt; to Exalt Is to Humble

The second reason this secret wisdom is called a ladder is "because as the same steps of a ladder are used for both ascent and descent, so also the same communications produced by this secret contemplation extol [us] in God and humiliate [us] within [ourselves]." However, unlike a ladder, on which we are either ascending or descending, contemplation "simultaneously exalt[s] and humble[s] [us]" (N 2.18.2). This refers to the inverse consequences of pride and humility that are hidden from us. When we choose to practice humility, we feel we are descending, but in reality we are being exalted. This is due to the fact that God's grace is purifying us of pride and helping us to grow in humility. Conversely, when we feel elated by an inordinate opinion of ourselves, we are descending into pride. These are examples of how we misinterpret our own experience and how John, our third-person omniscient narrator, discloses to us the spiritual reality beneath our erroneous, emotional interpretation.

The Ups and Downs of Contemplation

Naturally speaking, and disregarding the spiritual, which it does not feel, the soul, if it desires to pay close attention, will clearly recognize how on this road it suffers many ups and downs, and how immediately after prosperity some tempest and trial follows, so much so that seemingly the calm was given to forewarn and strengthen it against the future penury. It sees, too, how abundance and tranquility succeed misery and torment, and in such a way that it thinks it was made to fast before celebrating that feast. This is the ordinary procedure in the state of contemplation until one arrives at the

quiet state: The soul never remains in one state, but everything is ascent and descent. (N 2.18.3)

Many of the ups and downs of life are the result of changing
circumstances; conversely, others are caused by the waxing and
waning of contemplation within our souls. John bids us to "pay
close attention" (N 2.18.3) to these workings of grace. By doing
so, we will realize two important truths. First, "immediately after
prosperity some tempest and trial follows" [that] will "forewarn
and strengthen [us] against the future penury" (N 2.18.3). In
knowing this fact, we will not be caught off guard by some interior trial or storm because when we are forewarned we are fore-
armed. Vigilance regarding an unexpected trial will keep us on an
even keel in the storms of life. As Marcus Aurelius writes, "The
art of living is more like wrestling than dancing[; it] demands a
firm and watchful stance against any unexpected onset."[1]

In consequence, during times of prosperity we can garner
strength to resist temptation during times of darkness. John
invites us to become conscious of the working of God's grace
as we ascend and descend the secret ladder of contemplation
and interpret our "ups" and "downs" from a spiritual perspective rather than from an emotional one.[2]

Second, realizing that "abundance and tranquility succeed
misery and torment" (N 2.18.3) provides us with the knowledge that sustains us during times of darkness, namely, "all
things are passing," as St. Teresa of Ávila wrote in her so-called
bookmark, lines found written in her breviary:

Let nothing disturb you,
Let nothing frighten you.
All things are passing.
God alone is changeless.

For Reflection

St. Augustine said that we often do not realize that we have grown in a specific virtue until we experience that we respond differently to a familiar situation. When we experience this growth, we are at a loss to explain how it happened. This is an example of what John means when he writes that "the soul neither knows nor understands how this comes to pass" (N 2.17.2). When you respond differently to a familiar situation, have you ever attributed this change to the work of "secret contemplation" (N 2.17.2)?

NIGHT 2.19–20

The Ladder of Love

At the end of chapter 18, John writes that he wishes to give "greater clarity" (N 2.18.5) to the image of the ladder. He does so in chapters 19 and 20 by listing ten successive steps (*grados*) or degrees of transformation. These steps represent an outline of the entire spiritual journey, from our first dissatisfaction with the things of this world to the beatific vision. The first five steps of the ladder of love is a brief summation of the transformation of desire that John has presented in *The Dark Night*, whereas the last five steps deal with the effects of transformation that he will write about toward the end of *The Dark Night* and in *The Spiritual Canticle*. With this perspective in mind, let us briefly summarize the ten steps.

STEP ONE

On the first step toward God, we lose our appetite for the things of this world. We become "unable then to find satisfaction, support, consolation, or a resting place in anything" (N 2.19.1). This loss is the work of God; it is the result of consolation given from above; it is the passive night; and it is what God does. "The soul does not get this sickness unless [it] is sent from above" (N 2.19.1). Like all expressions of conversion, this step is a turning from and a turning toward; our desire turns from the things of this world toward the things of God. There is a loss of appetite for the things of this world and a transformation of appetite for the things of God.

STEP TWO

This transformation of appetite for the things of God makes us "search for God" (N 2.19.2). This is manifested in two ways: we think and talk about God. "In all its thoughts it turns immediately to the Beloved; in all converse and business it at once speaks about the Beloved" (N 2.19.2). This step is the experience of being in love: all we think about and all we talk about is the person we love. However, when one is in love, thinking and talking are not enough. One wants to express one's love by *doing*.

STEP THREE

The "third step . . . prompts the soul to the performance of works and gives it fervor that it might not fail" (N 2.19.3). This step exhibits many of the characteristics of a "beginner" at the point at which God withdraws consolation (see N 1.12). It "feels that it does little . . . [and it is] really worse than others. . . . It is far removed from vainglory, presumption, and the practice of condemning others" (N 2.19.3).

STEP FOUR

The fourth step "is very elevated" (N 2.19.4) because an important transformation has taken place. In spite of a lack of consolation, an "unwearisome suffering is engendered" (N 2.19.4) in the will. This indicates that a shift in psychic energy has occurred in the will. We no longer seek "consolation or satisfaction either in God or in anything else" (N 2.19.4). We no longer count the cost of loving. We "pursue God in the spirit of suffering for his sake" (N 2.19.4). Our ability to do God's will is becoming less dependent upon affect.

STEP FIVE

As we become detached from seeking ourselves and more attached to seeking God, we are raised to the fifth step. Here, we long to possess the object of our love with "an impatient desire" (N 2.19.5). This "impatient" desire is true patience; it manifests the strength to bear "delay" (N 2.19.5). We become detached from seeking the things of this world and are willing to wait for the world to come. We have been given the strength to live in hope, bearing the tension of being stranded between two worlds, one dying, and the other powerless to be born. We suffer the present time, waiting for future glory to be revealed, groaning in labor, and waiting to give birth (Rom 8:18, 22).

John says that this is the "step of hunger" on which the soul "feeds on love" (N 2.19.5) because the act of love is the willingness to wait. In consequence, the soul expands. As St. Augustine writes, "God by deferring our hope, stretches our desire; by the desiring stretches the mind [and] makes it more capacious."[1]

STEP SIX

On the sixth step, we take a quantum leap; we enter a new world; and we have given birth to the fruits of our labors. The tension of living in hope that was endured on the fifth step has been transformed into the joyous expectation of hope on the sixth. The quality of our response to God has been transformed; we have acquired "that spiritual agility and vivacity . . . and the readiness in performing charitable actions," writes St. Francis de Sales.[2] The joyous alacrity and sprightliness of a person on this step "makes the soul run swiftly [*liger-amente*—swiftly or lightly] toward God and experience many touches in him. And it runs without fainting by reason of its hope. The love that has invigorated it makes it fly swiftly. [Or as] the prophet Isaiah [writes] . . . *They shall take wings like the eagle and shall fly* [Is 40:31]" (N 2.20.1).

To understand the nature of this eager joy, let us compare it to the joy that is given to beginners by means of consolation. The grace of consolation is really a catalyst. It provides the impetus that spurs us to love; it is a "jump start." Though consolation is a gift from God, it is a gift "on loan," which will be taken back in due time.

In contrast, the eager joy native to the sixth step is the affective manifestation of charity that has united us to God; it is the fruit of transformation. As St. Thomas Aquinas writes, "The necessary result of the love of charity is joy; because every lover rejoices at being united to the beloved" ST I–II, q. 70, a. 3).

STEP SEVEN

Just because we have gained the capacity to respond swiftly on the sixth step, this does not mean that our response is not costly. On the contrary, it is precisely because we do not hesitate to do God's will that we respond more frequently and in situations that are strange and unfamiliar to us. By doing so, our response is enlarged; it becomes magnanimous. In this regard, John quotes the psalmist. "*I have run the way of your commandments, when you enlarged my heart* [Ps 119:32]" (N 2.20.1).

The opposite of the joy of magnanimity is the depressive sadness of *acedia*, the sadness of a shrunken soul that has become tightfisted in its response to God. The soul is depressed, living within its cramped quarters and fearful to venture beyond the walls of its confinement.[3]

The sprightly joy exhibited on the sixth step is due partly to being released from our confinement; we have "sprouted wings" and are released from our cage. The spacious magnanimity is manifested on the seventh step as "ardent boldness" and "ardent daring" (N 2.20.2) because we are not hindered by three forms of fear. "At this stage love neither profits by the judgment to wait nor makes use of the counsel to retreat, [nor] can it be curbed through shame (*vergüenza*)" (N 2.20.2). Let us consider each in turn.

They Do Not Profit by the Judgment to Wait

When we speak of a person who has made an imprudent choice, we often think of someone who has plunged into a course of action without looking at the facts. He or she has made a choice without taking due counsel or has formed a judgment without sufficient consideration.

However, there is another type of imprudent person, the one who deliberates too much. These people are so filled with fearful circumspection that they are unwilling to act unless they have absolute certitude that they will be safe before venturing forth.

People on the seventh step do not engage in this second form of imprudence. They know that they cannot "profit by the judgment to wait" (N 2.20.2). They do not procrastinate when they know they must act; they willingly venture beyond the frontier of the familiar, with "ardent boldness" (N 2.20.2). They are willing to make mistakes in the eyes of the world in the process of doing God's will. They know that God's foolishness is wiser than the wisdom of men.

They Do Not Make Use of the Counsel to Retreat

One of the most famous rationalizations for cowardice in English literature is found in Shakespeare's play *Henry IV*, part 1. There, Falstaff feigns death on a battlefield in order to avoid combat. At the end of his cynical, flippantly witty, self-justifying monologue, Falstaff delivers the oft-quoted line, "The better part of valor is discretion" (act 5, scene 4, line 121). His speech embodies what St. Thomas calls "the false prudence of the sage" (*On the Book of Job* 8.1) or the "prudence of the flesh" (ST II, II, q. 47, a. 13), which is sagacity in the service of "safety first."

When we are afraid, not only do we tend to procrastinate, but also we are tempted to escape what we fear. If our fear could speak, it would say, "Get me out of this!" In such a state of mind, we hope that someone will be able to talk us out of doing what we fear. At such moments, we are vulnerable to "the false prudence of the sage"; we are tempted to make use of counsel to retreat. But people on the seventh step don't give into this temptation. They neither ask for such advice nor follow it when it is offered.

They Are Not Curbed in the Face of Shame (*Vergüenza*)

"To feel shame is to feel seen in a painfully diminished sense," writes psychologist Gershen Kaufman.[4] Those on the seventh step are willing to be diminished in the eyes of others for the sake of God. *Vergüenza* includes being shamed, disgraced, dishonored, or embarrassed. These individuals find their security in God. Their self-esteem is not dependent upon what other people think of them; therefore, they do not cower in fear before the onslaught of public opinion.

However, although they disregard public opinion, they are not rude or disdainful of social norms. Their "ardent boldness" (N 2.20.2) does not transform them into self-proclaimed and boorish prophets. They are protected from psychic inflation by humility. "On these steps [the soul] must always conserve humility" (N 2.20.2).[5]

They do not "become daring [unless they] perceive the divine favor of the king's scepter held out toward [them]" (N 2.20.2). In short, their words and actions are ruled and regulated by God. Like Jesus, they can say, "The word you hear is not mine, but is from the Father who sent me" (Jn 14:24).

STEP EIGHT

This step roughly corresponds to the spiritual betrothal by which a soul is united to God, but not completely. It suffers the incompleteness of its own being; it pines only for God to make it whole, and in consequence, "everything wearies it" (IC 5.2.8). This state of holy dissatisfaction, which both John and St. Teresa refer to as the "wound," is one of the most painful purgations. All of us experience this form of suffering many times in the dark night but not to this degree.

STEP NINE

In chapter 10 of book two of *The Dark Night*, John compares spiritual transformation to the effects that fire has on a log. The goal of spiritual transformation is union with God in which the soul and God are one—"the fire transforms the wood into itself" (N 2.10.1). In *The Living Flame of Love*, John uses the same image in describing union. "The fire has penetrated the wood, transformed it, and united it with itself" (F Prol 3).

On step nine, souls have become completely transformed into God. The image that John uses to describe this union is that of a glowing ember that pulsates softly and quietly. Their "love causes [these souls] to burn gently." They "burn gently in God," which produces a "gentle and delightful ardor" (N 2.20.4).

What burns gently is their ardor. Thus, we encounter in them a gentleness that is strong and a strength that is gentle. They personify the words of St. Francis de Sales: "Nothing is so strong as gentleness; nothing is so gentle as real strength."

STEP TEN

One way of thinking about the first nine steps of John's ladder of love is to see them as our growing capacity to receive God. For this is the nature of the dark night. "This dark night is an inflow of God into the soul" (N 2.5.1). We will fully obtain the capacity to look upon the face of God only in eternity. On the tenth step, the soul has entered eternal life. "[It] is no longer of this life" (N 2.20.4).

We are transformed into the reality upon which we gaze. "Love assimilates the soul to God completely because of the clear vision of God that [it] possesses. . . . This vision is the cause of the soul's complete likeness to God," by which it becomes "God through participation" (N 2.20.5).

All of our choices entail consequences, which cumulatively result in the person that we become. All of us are transformed into what we most consistently love because "love effects a likeness between the lover and the loved" (A 1.4.3).

For Reflection

Have you ever been tempted to make use of the "counsel to retreat" (N 2.20.2)?

In short, have you ever deliberately asked someone for advice, knowing the person you asked would most probably give you the answer you wanted to hear?

Conversely, have you been given the grace of "ardent daring" (N 2.20.2), to ask a wise person for advice whom you knew would tell you the truth you needed to hear?

NIGHT 2.21

Departing in Disguise

⤳∽⤳

T he theological virtues of faith, hope, and charity are three
modes of God's self-communication that so transform us
that there exists "a likeness between the lover and the loved" (A
1.4.3). These virtues are not objects that we can put on as we
put on clothing; rather, they are qualities of soul by which we
partake of the divine nature. In spite of this fact, John symbolizes the theological virtues as the three-layered vesture worn by
medieval knights. The innermost garment was a white, quilted
cotton coat called a gambeson (faith). Over the gambeson a
suit of chain mail armor called a hauberk (hope) was put on.
The outer covering of the knight's vesture was a heraldic sur-
coat (charity).[1]

The purpose of John's symbolism is to draw our attention
to one aspect of the theological virtues: their protective quality. The inner white tunic of faith protects the intellect from
the devil's wiles; the green mail coat of hope defends memory
from the temptations of the world; and the outer red toga of
charity conceals the will from the allurements of the flesh.

As we deal with the three vestures of the soul individually,
we must keep in mind their intrinsic unity. Just as the faculties
of intellect, memory, and will are dependent upon one another
for their operation, so too the theological virtues of faith,

hope, and love grow in unison (A 3.1.1). The intrinsic unity of the theological virtues may be expressed in three ways: a loving, hopeful faith; a faithful, loving hope; and a faithful, hopeful love. There is a similar unity regarding the three enemies of the soul: the world, the flesh, and the devil. "In the weakening of one, the other two are weakened also" (Pre 3).

THE INNER WHITE TUNIC OF FAITH

Faith is neither a mental stance by which we adopt theological propositions as being true nor an opinion held by the mind. It is an experiential knowledge of God. "The likeness between faith and God is so close that no other difference exists than that between believing in God and seeing him" (A 2.9.1). In short, the white garment of faith is our innermost vision of reality by which we perceive, discern, and judge all things in the light of God's grace. Faith as gift is the divine horizon upon which we receive true self-knowledge and are able to correctly appraise the worth of the world. Faith as response is our steadfast contemplative gaze.

Let us recall John's advice regarding the gift of contemplation. He says that because God's presence as contemplation is as delicate as "air that escapes when one tries to grasp it in one's hand" (N 1.9.6), we need to develop the capacity to be quiet and gently attend to the divine presence. This growing capacity is faith, for "faith . . . is a habit of soul" (A 2.3.1) by which we acquire a habitual consciousness of God. The fruit of this habit is twofold. First, we are able to "delicately experience the interior nourishment [of God's presence]" (N 1.9.6). Second, because we have become highly attuned to the delicate inflow of God, we have also become attuned to any movement within ourselves that is not of God. This heightened sensitivity to evil is particularly important in protecting us from the wiles of the devil, our "most astute enemy" (N 2.21.4).

The Devil

Because the devil is "astute" (N 2.21.4) and "adept" (A 3.11.5) at "deceiving [the soul] under the appearance of the good" (Pre 10) with "skilled deception" (IC 5.4.8), we need the discerning sensitivity of faith. Faith bestows upon us the discriminating knowledge by which we instinctively know when something is not of God. This is why "faith gives [us] strong protection . . . against the devil (N 2.21.4). Consequently, we are not easily deceived by the subtle temptations of the devil. However, faith as contemplation is insufficient for spiritual progress for two reasons. First, although faith grants vision, it does not bestow the desire to seek what the vision discloses. Second, just being aware of temptation is not the same as having the strength to resist it. Both the desire to seek what faith discloses and the strength to resist temptation are provided by the theological virtue of hope.

THE GREEN MAIL COAT OF HOPE

The virtue of hope protects us from the "world," that is, from all the values and forces in society or a culture that are either hostile or antithetical to the values of the Gospel. Since the world is extrinsic to us and attacks us from "the outside," so to speak, John symbolizes the protection that hope provides as a "coat of mail" (N 2.21.6). Just as coats of mail shielded knights' bodies from the weapons of their enemies, so too hope shields us from the world's poison darts.

Why are we so vulnerable to the world's values? The answer lies in the dynamics of desire. By desire, I am referring not to appetites and needs that are biologically preconditioned but rather to what our culture tells us that we need.

The Mimetic Nature of Desire

For many years, French Catholic literary critic, philosopher, and historian René Girard studied the works of Flaubert, Stendhal, Dostoyevsky, Cervantes, and Proust. He discovered that as these authors matured and gained greater insight into human nature, they all came to the same conclusion regarding the nature of desire, namely, that it is mimetic, or imitative.[2] In short, our desires are evoked by the desires of others; we want something because other people want it. Or as Samuel Johnson puts it, "We catch from example the contagion of desire."[3] Let us take a simple example. One day a man takes his two children to his office. In the process of cleaning out his desk, he gives the discarded items to his children as gifts. He gives his son an old wall calendar with photos of nature scenes. The boy looks at the calendar for a few minutes and then throws it into the wastebasket. His sister retrieves it, looks at the photographs, and proclaims excitedly, "These are beautiful, so beautiful!" Instantly, her brother shouts, "Give it to me; it's mine; it's mine!"

This scenario is enacted countless times throughout our lives. One moment we don't want something, and the next moment we feel it is absolutely essential for our happiness. All that's needed for such a mysterious transformation to take place is for us to realize that it is desired by others. Mimetic desire is "contagious" and can cause a "veritable frenzy."[4]

The entire marketing industry is based upon mimetic desire. Companies produce commercials showing happy people using their product. The message is, if you want to be happy, you have to buy their product. We are constantly being told what we have to possess in order to be a success; how we have to look in order to be beautiful; and how we have to dress in order to be fashionable. If movie stars and professional models had potbellies, then none of us would be doing sit-ups or stomach crunches in order to develop washboard abs. If all celebrities bought their clothes at Walmart, then clothing that displays a Walmart logo prominently would be a fashion craze.

The deep need to be accepted and the fear of being rejected are powerful forces. They form an unconscious conspiracy that makes us believe we want what we don't want and feel what we don't feel. The more we become assimilated into "The World," the more we become a stranger to ourselves, even to the extent that we are not sure why we enjoy something.

We find an example of this effect in Sinclair Lewis's novel *Babbitt.* George F. Babbitt epitomizes the "man of the world," who has achieved the "American Dream." Babbitt possessed everything that society dictated was necessary for him to be a success. However, he didn't know whether he "enjoyed his sleeping-porch because of the fresh air or because it was the standard thing to have a sleeping-porch."[5] Babbitt believed he was "finding his place in [the world. But in reality] it was finding its place in him."[6]

Mimetic desire, combined with the fear of rejection, the need for acceptance, and the drive to distinguish ourselves, is a lethal combination. It makes us vulnerable to becoming so absorbed in worldly pursuits that the sum total of our hopes and dreams can become limited to this life alone. The virtue of hope, that "coat of mail" (N 2.21.6), protects us from our vulnerability to "becom[ing] absorbed in any worldly thing" by "elevat[ing] the soul to the things of eternal life" (N 2.21.6).

Hope elevates us by "rais[ing our] eyes to look only at God" (N 2.21.7), which is a metaphorical way of saying that hope transforms and redirects our desires to seek God as our final good. As this transformation takes place, our energy is transferred from pursuing the things of this world to pursuing the things of God. In consequence, we recognize earthly things for what "they truly are, dry, withered, dead and worthless" (N 2.21.6). In short, our desire for earthly things begins to wither and die. This is purely the work of God's grace; however, we can dispose ourselves for this transformation to take place. In this regard, we might ask the question, "What can we do to protect ourselves against our vulnerability to the 'World' or our susceptibility to mimicking the desires of others?" C. S. Lewis has a suggestion: enjoy what you like.

In *The Screwtape Letters*, Screwtape, the senior devil, advises his young trainee devil Wormwood to try to prevent his "client" from doing the things that he likes because such behavior can protect him from the temptations of the world.

> The deepest likings and impulses of any man are the raw material, the starting point, with which the Enemy [God] has furnished him. To get him away from those is therefore always a point gained; even in things indifferent it is always desirable to substitute the standards of the World, or convention, or fashion, for a human's own real likings. . . . The man who truly and disinterestedly enjoys any one thing in the world, for its own sake, and without caring twopence what other people say about it, is by that very fact forearmed against some of our subtlest modes of attack. You should always try to make the patient abandon the people or food or books he really likes in favour of the "best" people, the "right" food, the "important" books. I

have known a human defended from strong temptations to social ambition by a still stronger taste for tripe and onions.[7]

There is much here to ponder. All of us have been shaped by the conventions, fashions, and standards of the world to the extent that we sometimes forego what gives us joy. What a tragedy it is when our need to either be accepted by others or appear sophisticated overpowers our desire to enjoy the innocent pleasures of God's creation.

Hope and Memory

It may strike us as odd that John connects hope with memory, since hope orients us toward the future and memory roots us in the past. However, upon reflection, we realize that our dreams of who we strive to become are rooted in past experiences, all of which are recorded in memory. The person we strive and hope to become is shaped by key moments and early life choices. Psychiatrist Alfred Adler says that all of us have a guiding self-ideal, a fictional final goal for which we strive, which is shaped by early life choices. Adler said that if we examine a person's earliest memories, they will answer the questions, "What is this individual's aim? What is his conception of himself and of life?"[8]

Let's take the example of Father Griffin Smith. Ever since he could remember, he had wanted to become a priest. Though God had planted this desire in his heart, it became infected with an obsession to become a bishop. One evening when Griffin was seven years old, his parents were out of town and Griffin was spending the week at the home of his maternal grandparents. Griffin both loved and admired his grandfather. He was a kind, gentle retired English professor, who supported Griffin in his desire to become a priest. Griffin used to love to sit with his grandfather in his den, listening to him tell stories from the great works of literature.

One night, his grandfather told him how he came to be called Griffin. He had suggested the name to his daughter when she was pregnant. He told her it was a very sacred and noble name, for in Dante's *Purgatorio*, the Griffin was a symbol of Christ. "Perhaps," his grandfather said, "with a name like yours, one day you may become a bishop, for doesn't St. Paul say somewhere that it is a noble thing to aspire to be a bishop?" Griffin was deeply moved by what his grandfather had said.

The following week, Griffin was in the sacristy of his parish church getting dressed to serve Mass. The pastor was late that morning. As Griffin sat quietly, waiting for the pastor to arrive, he began to stare at a large painting of a bishop that hung upon the wall. The bishop's countenance was serene, and his bearing was regal, which together personified self-possession. The portrait began to hold an uncanny power over Griffin. He would frequently "make a visit" to the portrait and sit quietly before it as one would before the Blessed Sacrament. Then he would go home and stand in front of the bathroom mirror, trying to re-create the look that he had seen in the bishop's face. Griffin never forgot "his" bishop; he personified who Griffin wanted to become.

After ordination, Father Griffin became well known in his diocese and well liked among his fellow priests. He volunteered to serve on every diocesan committee imaginable, and his name or photo appeared frequently in the diocesan newspaper. On his day off, he offered to celebrate Masses in various parishes in order to relieve his fellow priests of some of their work.

Griffin drove himself to maintain a high profile in his diocese to achieve his goal. However, he paid a high price for visibility. His nonstop lifestyle took its toll. He became drained physically, mentally, emotionally, and spirituality. One day, in this depleted condition, he attended the priests' convocation for his diocese and overheard two priests talking about him. "I don't think I've ever seen a worse case of 'scarlet fever' than I have in Griffin. I can't believe that he doesn't realize how blatantly evident it is to everyone."[9]

Griffin was humiliated and devastated by what he heard. In a flash of self-knowledge, he realized that he was pursuing a phantom. Within a week he was hospitalized for exhaustion, which proved to be a severe mercy. It provided him with time to think and pray. During his hospitalization, he had a long talk with his bishop, who was the first person to whom Griffin had ever revealed his life's story. This disclosure gave Griffin the permission he needed to stop his frantic behavior. He resigned from several diocesan committees and stopped helping out in neighboring parishes. At first, he did not find the changes difficult because he didn't have the strength to do anything beyond his parish duties. However, as he regained his vitality, Griffin's old dream began to reassert itself. What he had to do was unambiguously clear. He had to restrain himself from giving into his compulsion. When we stop feeding something it begins to die.

Griffin's hope of becoming a bishop had to wither and die so that a new hope could be born. Then "memory is not trapped within the limits of personal history, but has attained its proper function of growth and self-transcendence," as Carmelite scholar Ross Collings, O.C.D., writes.[10]

THE RED LIVERY OF CHARITY

Where we find our joy is ultimately the measure of who we become because joy is the fulfillment of desire. The soul's movement to find its joy in God is charity, writes St. Augustine. "What I mean by charity or love is any urge of the spirit to find joy in God for his own sake, and in oneself and one's neighbor for God's sake." Conversely, Augustine defines "the flesh" or cupidity as the movement of the soul to find its joy apart from God. "By cupidity [I mean] any impulse of the spirit to find joy in oneself and one's neighbor, and in any kind of bodily thing at all, not for the sake of God."[11] It is charity that protects us from our inclination toward self-centered love. As John writes, "With this livery of charity . . . the soul receives protection and concealment from the flesh, her third enemy. For where there is true love of God, love of self and of one's own things finds no entry" (N 2.21.10).

One of the fruits of charity is joy that provides us with protection. St. Thomas Aquinas writes that "the sequel of charity is joy" and "the perfection of joy is peace" by which we "cannot be disquieted" (ST I–II, q. 70, a. 3). As Scripture has it, "the joy of the Lord is your strength" (Neh 8:10). The deep spiritual happiness that charity provides protects us from seeking our solace in the "flesh," which leads to misery.

Self-love cannot worm its way into the heart that truly loves God because love makes us beautiful, and beauty, as St. Thomas teaches, is that quality of goodness that satisfies desire (ST I–II, q. 27, a. 1). In consequence, the qualities that charity bestows, "elegance . . . loveliness and charm" (N 2.21.10), so satisfy the soul that it is protected from seeking its joy in things that are less than God.

For Reflection

Where do you see mimetic desire operating most strongly in your life?

Where do you feel the most pressure to conform to the latest fad or fashion?

Have you ever considered that the weariness you feel in attempting to conform to the prevailing trends of this world is the result of God's grace operating in your life that enables you to recognize that the things of this world are "truly dry, withered, dead and worthless" (N 2.21.6)?

NIGHT 2.22–24

My House Being Now All Stilled

~⊃⌒~

Chapter 22 consists of only two paragraphs. Paragraph 1 concludes the previous chapter; it speaks of the freedom that a person has gained from departing from the influence of the devil, the world, and the flesh. Paragraph 2 summarizes John's intention in writing *The Dark Night of the Soul*.

> What was more important and the reason I undertook this task was to explain this night to many souls who in passing through it do not understand it, as is pointed out in the prologue. The nature of this night has now been explained to some extent. We have also discussed the many blessings this night brings to the soul—though in a way that makes them seem less than what they in fact are—and how great a grace it is for one who passes through it. We have written of these blessings so that when souls become frightened by the horror of so many trials they might take courage in the sure hope of the many advantageous blessings obtained from God through these trials. (N 2.22.2)

This succinct summary of *The Dark Night of the Soul* would lead us to believe that John has come to the end of his labors and has no more to say on his subject. Yet immediately he launches out on his most comprehensive analysis of the meddling of the devil. Why John singles out the devil from the other two enemies of the soul for special consideration is not clear. Perhaps he felt that since the dangers of the flesh and the world were self-evident, no further explanation was needed.

In contrast, since the devil is the most "astute" (N 2.21.4) and "adept" (A 3.11.5) at "deceiving [us] under the appearance of the good" (Pre 10), John may have felt that more counsel was required. Whatever the case may be, in chapter 23, John connects his main teaching on the interference of the devil with contemplation, that is, God's presence that teaches "secretly and instructs [the soul] in the perfection of love without its doing anything or understanding how this happens" (N 2.5.1).

CONTEMPLATION: THE SOUL'S SECURITY

To understand what we must do in order to protect ourselves from the wiles of the devil, let us compare the advice that St. Teresa of Ávila gives to those who are experiencing the prayer of quiet with John's advice to people who are receiving contemplation. Their advice is similar.

The prayer of quiet (a degree of contemplation) is like sitting in the eye of a hurricane. As the will is captivated by and anchored in the quiet of God's presence, the mind swirls about, spinning off images and ideas. "The soul will be in the greatest quiet and the intellect will be . . . distracted" (W 31.8). Teresa says that this situation resembles a person [the will] sitting quietly in one's home, while a "madman" [the mind] is making a commotion as he runs around the house. Teresa's advice is that we "shouldn't pay any more attention to the intellect than [we] would to a madman" (W 31.8).

226 THE DARK NIGHT

The danger, says Teresa, is that we will be tempted to leave our house in order to subdue the madman. However, if we do so, we will fail to subdue the mind, and in the process, we will lose the quiet that God is giving to us. "If the will goes out to fight with the intellect so as to give a share of the experience, by drawing the intellect after itself, it cannot do so at all; [and it will] lose that divine nourishment [that God is giving it]" (W 31.9).

Just as Teresa advises us not to go out and engage the intellect in battle, so too John counsels us to guard ourselves from being drawn out into the "outer world," that is, "the exterior and interior faculties [imagination] of the sensory part of the soul" (N 2.23.2). This is because it is only by means of sensible impressions and mental images that the devil can tempt us. The devil "cannot reach the soul" (N 2.23.2); he cannot cross the threshold from sense to spirit.

He is like Dracula, who is powerless to cross a threshold uninvited, so he lures unsuspecting victims into his domain. When Jonathan Harker arrives at Dracula's castle, Dracula opens the door but does not come forward. "'Welcome to my house! Enter freely and of your own free will!' He made no motion of stepping to meet me, but stood like a statue, as though his gesture of welcome had fixed him into stone. The instant, however, that I stepped over the threshold, he moved impulsively forward, and holding out his hand grasped mine with a strength which made me wince, an effect which was not lessened by the fact that it seemed as cold as ice—more like the hand of a dead man than a living man."[1]

Later in the story, Dracula's strange behavior is explained. He can neither force a person to enter his castle nor cross a threshold unless he is given permission. "He may not enter anywhere . . . unless there be someone of the household who bids him to come."[2]

Likewise, because the devil "cannot reach" (N 2.23.2) into the soul's inner sanctuary, where communications between God and ourselves take place, he tries to draw us out of our center into his own domain: the memory, imagination, and the senses. For there, his weapons of deception are powerful.

The devil is defeated when we do not engage him in combat—when we remain centered in God and do not allow ourselves to become ensnared in the thoughts and images of our minds. This is what it means to be "in concealment" (N 2.23.1) and to "remain in darkness" (N 2.23.3). The reason John counsels us to sequester ourselves from the clamor of our thoughts and the clutter of our imaginings is not solely to protect ourselves from the wiles of the devil but also "so that there may be room [within ourselves] for a more abundant spiritual communication" (N 2.23.3). Quieting one's heart is at the core of John's spirituality because "God is received in divine silence" (SLL 28) in which "God teaches the soul secretly and instructs it in the perfection of love" (N 2.5.1).

THE DEVIL AS ENVIOUS OUTSIDER

At the end of *The Screwtape Letters*, Wormwood's patient is killed in the London Blitz. Wormwood stands on the sidelines, an impotent observer, witnessing his patient communing with heavenly beings. Screwtape says to Wormwood,

> As he saw you, he also saw *Them*. I know how it was. You reeled back dizzy and blinded, more hurt by them than he had ever been by bombs. The degradation of it!—that this thing of earth and slime could stand upright and converse with spirits before whom you, a spirit, could only cower. Perhaps you had hoped that the awe and strangeness of it

would dash his joy. But that is the cursed thing; the gods are strange to mortal eyes, and yet they are not strange. He had no faintest conception till that very hour of how they would look, and even doubted their existence. But when he saw them he knew that he had always known them and realized what part each one of them had played at many an hour in his life when he had supposed himself alone, so that now he could say to them, one by one, not "Who are you?" but "So it was you all the time." All that they were and said at this meeting woke memories. The dim consciousness of friends about him which had haunted his solitudes from infancy was now at last explained; that central music in every pure experience which had always just evaded memory was now at last recovered. Recognition made him free of their company almost before the limbs of his corpse became quiet. *Only you were left outside.*[3] (italics added)

This is the situation of the devil in John's text. He is an outsider who can no longer share the intimate communications that the soul enjoys. He is like someone standing outside a locked room who can hear only muffled voices from within. "The devil is ignorant of the nature of these very interior and secret spiritual communications [that the soul is experiencing but] perceives that [it] is receiving them because of the great quietude and silence [that they cause] in the sensory part [of the soul]" (N 2.23.4).

The devil is a spoiler, who out of the impotent rage of envy tries "to wreak on innocent frail man his loss"[4] and prevent the soul from enjoying the sweet communications that it is receiving. "Since he is aware that he cannot impede [these communications] in the depths of the soul, he does everything possible to excite and disturb the sensory part, which he can affect with sufferings, horrors, and fears. He intends by this agitation to disquiet . . . the soul in its reception and enjoyment of that good" (N 2.23.4).

However, the devil's attempt to disturb the soul often recoils upon his head, for when the soul begins to experience the agitation that the devil is arousing, it instinctively withdraws into its inner sanctuary. "In experiencing the troublesome presence of the enemy, the soul enters more deeply into its inner depths without knowing how and without any efforts of its own, and it is sharply aware of being placed in a certain refuge where it is more hidden and withdrawn from the enemy." (N 2.23.4)

We have a symbol of the soul's instinctive gravitation toward its inner depths in Miloš Forman's film adaptation of Peter Shaffer's play *Amadeus* in the scene where Mozart and his wife, Constance, are visited by Mozart's father, Leopold. One morning, Leopold is criticizing Constance for her housekeeping. Constance becomes enraged and begins to scream at Leopold. Leopold is infuriated. As the shouting escalates, Mozart withdraws quietly into another room. As he closes the door, the outer cacophony fades in the background as we hear Mozart's music arising from within his soul. Mozart instinctively knew where to find shelter for his soul. He withdrew into his inner depths. We too should withdraw into our inner sanctuary when we begin to experience the disrupting presence of the enemy.

The activity of the soul is a response to its receptivity. It "enter[s] more deeply into its inner depths" as it experiences itself "being placed in a certain refuge" (N 2.23.4). Withdrawing and being "withdrawn" (N 2.23.4) have become two aspects of the same reality. This "instinctive affinity" between the soul and God is the fruit of contemplation, which John has discussed throughout *The Dark Night*.

Let us recall that when God first withdraws us from discursive meditation into contemplative prayer, we are so unaccustomed to contemplation that we must be exhorted "to persevere patiently . . . to remain in rest and quietude" (N 1.10.3–4). As we persevere in resting in contemplation, we begin to make "within [ourselves] a peaceful place for [God]" (N 1.11.1). Over time, this peaceful place becomes our "home." "When the soul has become established in the quietude and solitary love of her Bridegroom . . . she is settled in God and God in her" (C 35.1). By means of God's quiet and solitary love, we are instinctively drawn and withdraw "deeply into [our] inner depths" (N 2.23.4), whenever the devil tries to disturb our peace.

THE EVIL THAT REFINES THE SOUL TO RECEIVE THE GOOD

Flower in the crannied wall,

I pluck you out of the crannies,

I hold you here, root and all, in my hand,

Little flower—but if I could understand

What you are, root and all, and all in all,

I should know what God and man is.[5]

This poem by Alfred Lord Tennyson can serve as a symbol of creation's relationship to God. We can only truly know any part of creation by tracing it back to its origin. Our quest down this long river of exploration would eventually empty us into the infinite ocean of God, the source and sustainer of all life. Thus, in coming to know Tennyson's flower, we would come to know God and ourselves, for God is the ground of all being.

Similarly, if we are to obtain "the rest and quietude [of our] spiritual home," we must come to dwell in our deepest center, where Creator and creature are united, where God is known as our sustainer and source. In our innermost substance, we experience God as our divine Source "by means of . . . substantial touches of divine union" (N 2.24.3).

In preparation for an experience of this supreme good, sometimes God allows us to be invaded by a "diabolic communication" (N 2.23.9), a "spiritual horror" (N 2.23.10) that is beyond description. It is not clear why God permits this. However, in order to give some explanation, John compares the experience of "spiritual horror" which precedes the experience of a "substantial touch" to the purpose of fasting on the vigil of a feast. The fasting is meant to heighten the joy of the feast. "It should be understood that when the good angel allows the devil the advantage of reaching the soul with this spiritual horror, he does so that it may be purified and prepared, through this spiritual vigil, for some great feast and spiritual favor" (N 2.23.10).

In short, the experience of one extreme is heightened by the experience of its opposite. Just as fasting cleanses and refines the palate, so too the "preceding horror of the evil spirit greatly refines the soul so it can receive this good" (N 2.23.10). Or as St. Augustine writes, an experience of "evil . . . sets the good in higher relief."[6] Thus, to prepare us to experience the "intimacy of God" (N 2.23.12), God sometimes allows us to experience abandonment.

John is not suggesting that we must experience the utter absence of God as a preparation to experience the fullness of God. However, the cry of Jesus upon the cross, "My God, my God, why have you forsaken me?" (Mt 27:46) will be the lot of some. Why this is so is buried in the eternal silence of God's providence.

For Reflection

One of the fruits of the dark night is that "the soul enters more deeply into its inner depths" (N 2.23.4). This is the result of grace alone. However, we can dispose ourselves to being placed in our inner depths by "persever[ing] patiently . . . to remain in rest and quietude" (N 1.10.3–4). The first step of remaining in quietude is being on guard against the things of this world that draw us out of the center of our souls. "I must guard against being withdrawn from this holy interior silence,"[7] writes St. Elizabeth of the Trinity, by practicing exterior silence.

What have you found helpful in practicing exterior silence?

NIGHT 2.25
Conclusion

The focus of *The Dark Night of the Soul* is God's grace, the "inflow of God into the soul" (N 2.5.1) that takes on many forms, be it consolation, peaceful contemplation, or dark contemplation. As John comes to the end of his work, he describes the chief characteristic of a soul that has been transformed by this divine inflow—peace.

The peace that John describes is captured by the following stanza of Thomas Gray's poem, "Elegy Written in a Country Churchyard."

> Far from the madding crowd's ignoble strife,
> Their sober wishes never learned to stray;
> Along the cool sequestered vale of life
> They kept the noiseless tenor of their way.[1]

We journey in peace, not because we are cut off from the world or disengaged from life but because we have become sequestered from the madding crowd of our clamorous appetites. No longer are we embroiled in the ignoble strife of sensuality and egotism. Thus, we do not stray from God. Rather, "God conducts [us] by so solitary and secret a contemplation, one so remote and alien to all the senses, that nothing pertinent to the senses, nor any touch of creature, can reach or detain [us] on the route leading to the union of love. Love alone . . . guides and moves [us] . . . in an unknown way along the road of solitude" (N 2.25.2, 4).

The road of solitude does not isolate us from others but leads us to serve the community. As St. Teresa writes of those who have reached divine union, "the calm these souls have interiorly is for the sake of their having much less calm exteriorly and much less desire to have exterior calm" (IC 7.4.10). "Prayer [is] not for the sake of our enjoyment but so as to have this strength to serve" (IC 7.4.12). Or as John puts it, the inflow of God "which purges [the soul] of its habitual ignorances and imperfections" does so in order that God can "teach the soul secretly . . . in the perfection of love" (N 2.5.1).

For Reflection

The goal of the spiritual journey that John sets before us in *The Dark Night of the Soul* is the fulfillment of the two great commandments: love God and love your neighbor. If you are allowing God to teach you in the perfection of love, then you can be assured that God is guiding you through the dark night. But if at times you find yourself resisting God's guidance, either because of fear or self-centeredness, do not be discouraged. God loves you and will never abandon you; God is always at your side, patiently waiting for you to continue your journey, which can begin at this very moment. "With what procrastination do you wait, since from this very moment you can love God in your heart" (SLL 87.26)?

NOTES

PREFACE

1. Bernard Cooke, *Sacraments and Sacramentality* (Mystic, Conn.: Twenty-Third Publications, 1983), 27–28.

ORIENTATION FOR THE READER

1. George H. Tavard, *Poetry and Contemplation in St. John of the Cross* (Athens: Ohio University Press, 1988), 56.

2. Louisa May Alcott, *A Modern Mephistopheles*, in *A Modern Mephistopheles and Taming a Tartar* (New York: Praeger, 1987), 24–25.

3. Anthony Storr, *Solitude: A Return to the Self* (New York: Ballantine, 1988), 174.

4. Charles Dickens, *A Christmas Carol* (New York: Bantam, 1986), 11.

5. Ibid., 11–12.

BOOK ONE

N 1.1. Introduction to the Imperfections of Beginners

1. Helen Merrell Lynd, *On Shame and the Search for Identity* (New York: Science Editions, 1958), 20.

N 1.2 Spiritual Pride

1. John Climacus, *The Ladder of Divine Ascent*, trans. Colm Luibheid and Norman Russell (New York: Paulist Press, 1982), 226.

2. Robert Louis Stevenson, *The Strange Case of Dr. Jekyll and Mr. Hyde* (New York: Dover, 1991), 42.

3. Oscar Wilde, *An Ideal Husband*, act 2 (New York: Dover, 2001).

4. Karen Horney, *Neurosis and Human Growth* (New York: Norton, 1950), 114–15.

5. Francis de Sales, *Introduction to the Devout Life*, trans. John K. Ryan (New York: Image Books, 1966), 149.

6. Jane Austen, *Pride and Prejudice* (New York: Bantam, 2003), 40.

7. George Eliot, *Middlemarch* (New York: Signet Classic, 1981), 15.

8. Ibid., 9.

9. Jerome, "Letters," in *The Writings of the Nicene and Post-Nicene Fathers*, vol. 6., trans. W. H. Fremantle, G. Lewis, and W. G. Martley, ed. Philip Schaff and Henry Wace (Grand Rapids, Mich.: Eerdmans, 1893), 93.

10. Augustine, *Commentary on the Lord's Sermon on the Mount*, trans. Denis J. Kavanagh, Fathers of the Church 11 (New York: Fathers of the Church, 1951), 149–50.

11. Blaise Pascal, *Thoughts of Blaise Pascal*, trans. Edward Craig (Boston: Gould, Kendall and Lincoln, 1849), 88–89.

12. Pride is a burden because it is a form of self-hate that sacrifices one's real self on the altar of an ideal self. From a psychological perspective, psychiatrist Karen Horney writes of the burden and damage that follows in the wake of what happens when one tries to actualize one's idealized self. "When an individual shifts his center of gravity to his idealized self," he will "despise" his real self. Since pride and self-hate are actually one entity." Horney, *Neurosis*, 110. *Neurosis and Human Growth* is an extremely penetrating, readable analysis of what Horney calls the "pride system." Her work can provide valuable insights into John's analysis of the faults of beginners.

13. Michel de Montaigne, "On the Cannibals," in *Four Essays*, trans. M. A. Screech (New York: Penguin, 1991), 16.

N 1.3. Spiritual Avarice

1. Josef Pieper, *The Four Cardinal Virtues*, trans. Daniel F. Coogan (New York: Harcourt Brace, 1965), 200–201.

2. For a good treatment of the differences among "religious life," "spiritual life," and "interior life," see Louis Bouyer's *Introduction to Spirituality*, trans. Mary Perkins Ryan (Collegeville, Minn.: Liturgical Press, 1961), 1–23.

3. T. S. Eliot, "Choruses from 'The Rock,'" in *Selected Poems* (New York: Harcourt Brace, 1964), 107.

NOTES ♦ **237**

N 1.4 Spiritual Lust

1. Francis de Sales, *Thy Will Be Done: Letters to Persons in the World*, trans. Henry Benedict Mackey (Manchester: Sophia Institute Press, 1995), 148.

2. *The Cloud of Unknowing and the Book of Privy Counseling*, trans. William Johnston, (Garden City, N.Y.: Image Books, 1973), 88.

3. Ibid.

4. In addition to the three main causes of sexual lust, John mentions, almost as an aside, a fourth cause. "If these impure thoughts and feelings arise from melancholia, individuals are not ordinarily freed from them until they are cured of that humor" (N 1.4.3). This is a psychologically astute observation, for hypersexuality is frequently a symptom of various affective disorders, most commonly, agitated depression and the manic phase of bipolar disorders.

5. T. S. Eliot, "Little Gidding," in *Four Quartets* (New York: Harcourt Brace Jovanovich, 1971), 54.

N 1.5 Spiritual Anger

1. Aquinas follows Aristotle's teaching that virtue is a mean between two extremes. In regard to anger, Aristotle teaches that meekness is the virtue that avoids the two extremes of irascibility and apathy. For Aristotle, meekness or gentleness is the virtue by which a person "gets angry at the right things and with the right people, and also in the right way and at the right time and for the right length of time." Aristotle, *The Ethics of Aristotle: The Nicomachean Ethics*, trans. J. A. K. Thomson (New York: Penguin, 1955), 160.

2. C. S. Lewis, *Mere Christianity* (New York: Macmillan, 1952), 76.

3. C. F. Kelley, *The Spirit of Love: Based on the Teachings of St. Francis de Sales* (New York: Harper, 1951), 196.

4. de Sales, *Thy Will be Done*, 169.

5. Ibid., 170.

6. Aristotle, *Ethics of Aristotle*, 160.

7. John Chrysostom, "Homilies on the Gospel of St. John and Hebrews," trans. Philip Schaff, Nicene and Post Nicene Fathers 14 (Grand Rapids, Mich.: Eerdmans, 1956), 20.

8. John Climacus, *The Ladder of Divine Ascent*, 146, 150.

9. Augustine, *Expositions of the Psalms*, vol. 6, trans. Maria Boulding (Hyde Park, N.Y.: New City Press, 2004), 306.

10. Augustine, *Letters 211–270*, trans. Roland Teske (Hyde Park, N.Y.: New City Press, 2005), 19 (letter 211).

N 1.6 Spiritual Gluttony

1. Robert Bolt, *A Man for All Seasons* (New York: Vintage, 1962), 43.

2. Aristotle, "The Nicomachean Ethics," in *The Basic Works of Aristotle*, ed. Richard McKeon, trans. W. B. Ross (New York: Random House, 1941), 1051.

3. Augustine, *The Confessions*, trans. F. J. Sheed (New York: Sheed & Ward, 1943), 41.

N 1.7 Spiritual Envy and Sloth

1. Dante, *Purgatorio*, 13.110–11, in *The Divine Comedy*, trans. John Ciardi (New York: Norton, 1970), 259.

2. Fyodor Dostoyevsky, *The Idiot*, trans. Constance Garnett (New York: Bantam Classics, 1983), 674.

3. Cyprian, "Jealousy and Envy," in *Saint Cyprian Treatises*, trans. Roy J. Deferrari (New York: Fathers of the Church, 1958), 298.

4. John Cassian, *The Institutes*, trans. Boniface Ramsey (New York: Newman Press, 2000), 210.

5. Augustine, *The Confessions*, trans. Maria Boulding (Hyde Park, N.Y.: New City Press, 1997), 198.

6. Sigmund Freud, *Mourning and Melancholia*, in *Psychodynamic Understanding of Depression*, ed. Willard Gaylin (New York: Jason Aronson, 1983), 57–58.

7. Anton Chekhov, *The Three Sisters*, in *Anton Chekhov: The Major Plays*, trans. Ann Dunnigan (New York: Signet Classics, 1964), 262.

8. T. S. Eliot, "The Dry Salvages," in *Four Quartets* (New York: Harcourt Brace Jovanovich, 1971), 44.

9. Wallace Stevens, "The Dwarf," in *The Collected Poems of Wallace Stevens* (New York: Knoff, 1954), 208.

10. Charles Dickens, *A Christmas Carol* (New York: Bantam, 1986), 22–23.

11. Ann and Barry Ulanov, *Cinderella and Her Sisters: The Envied and the Envying* (Philadelphia: Westminster Press, 1983), 21.

12. Frederick Faber, "The Monotony of Piety," in *Spiritual Conferences* (Philadelphia: Peter Reilly, 1957), 277.

13. William Wordsworth, "Lines Written a Few Miles above Tintern Abbey," in *William Wordsworth*, ed. Stephen Gill (Oxford: Oxford University Press, 1984), 132.

14. Augustine, *The Confessions*, trans. Maria Boulding, 187, 202.

N 1.9–10 The Withdrawal of Consolation

1. John Climacus, *The Ladder of Divine Ascent*, 76.

N 1.11 The Fire of Love

1. Augustine, *The Confessions*, trans. Vernon J. Bourke, Fathers of the Church 21 (New York: Fathers of the Church, 1953), 193–94.

2. For a good treatment on how to deal with distractions in prayer, see chapter 12, "Distractions Are for Healing," in *All Shall Be Well: The Spirituality of Julian of Norwich for Today*, by Robert Llewelyn (New York: Paulist Press, 1982), 106–16.

3. Robert Llewelyn, *A Doorway to Silence: The Contemplative use of the Rosary* (New York: Paulist Press, 1986), 20.

N 1.12 The Benefits of Self-Knowledge

1. Geneviève of the Holy Face (Céline Martin), *A Memoir of My Sister St. Thérèse*, trans. Carmelite Sisters of New York (New York: P. J. Kenedy & Sons, 1959), 138.

2. Benedicta Ward, *The Sayings of the Desert Fathers*, trans. Benedicta Ward (Kalamazoo, Mich.: Cistercian Publications, 1975), 141.

3. Francis de Sales, *Introduction to the Devout Life*, trans. John K. Ryan (New York: Image Books, 1966), 186.

N 1.14 The Trials of the Committed Soul

1. Much of the material in this chapter is taken from my article titled "Fair Is Foul and Foul Is Fair: An Interpretation of Chapter Fourteen of Book One of *The Dark Night of the Soul* of St. John of the Cross," in *A Better Wine: Essays Celebrating Kieran Kavanaugh, O.C.D.*, ed. Kevin Culligan (Washington, D.C.: ICS Publications, 2007), 63–93.

2. C. S. Lewis, "After Ten Years," in *The Dark Tower and Other Stories* (New York: Harcourt Brace Jovanovich, 1977), 137.

3. For two good studies on the lifting of repression in the dark night, see the following works by Michael Washburn: *The Ego and the Dynamic Ground: A Transpersonal Theory of Human Development* (Albany: State University of New York Press, 1995); and *Transpersonal Psychology in Psychoanalytic Perspective* (Albany: State University of New York Press, 1994).

4. Carl Jung, "The Relationship between the Ego and the Unconscious," in *Two Essays on Analytical Psychology* (New York: Princeton University Press, 1966), 169.

5. Jean-Pierre de Caussade, *Self-Abandonment to Divine Providence*, trans. P. H. Ramière (Springfield, Ill.: Templegate, 1959), 100.

6. Marie-Louise von Franz, *Puer Aeternus* (Boston: Sigo Press, 1981), 112–13.

7. Geneviève of the Holy Face (Céline Martin), *A Memoir of My Sister St. Thérèse*, 67.

8. Paul Tillich, *The Dynamics of Faith* (New York: Harper, 1957), 22.

9. Mark Twain, *The Adventures of Huckleberry Finn* (New York: Bantam, 1982), 85.

10. Ibid., 89.

11. Joseph W. Ciarrocchi, *The Doubting Disease: Help for Scrupulosity and Religious Compulsions* (Mahwah, N.J.: Paulist Press, 1995), 15.

12. David Fleming, *The Spiritual Exercises of St. Ignatius: A Literal Translation and a Contemporary Reading* (St. Louis, Mo.: Institute of Jesuit Sources, 1978), 229.

BOOK TWO

N 2.4 The Impact of Contemplation

1. Hein Blommestijn, Jos Huls, and Kees Waaijman, *The Footprints of Love: John of the Cross as Guide in the Wilderness*, trans. John Vriend (Leuven, Belgium: Peeters, 2000), 90.

2. C. S. Lewis, "The Shoddy Lands," in *The Dark Tower and Other Stories* (New York: Harcourt Brace Jovanovich, 1977),105.

3. Ibid., 105–6.

4. Ibid., 111.

N 2.5–6 Illumination and Purgation

1. The Spanish word *inmersión* is most commonly translated as immersion. However, it can also refer to a planet entering the shadow of a larger planet during an eclipse. Although John may not have had this meaning in mind, it is an apt symbol of the soul entering the dark night. It has entered into the sphere of an overwhelming presence.
2. Francis Thompson, "The Hound of Heaven," in *The Complete Poetical Works of Francis Thompson* (New York: Boni and Liveright, 1913), 277.
3. Thomas Hardy, "In Tenebris II," in *The Complete Poems: Poems of the Past and Present* (New York: Macmillan, 1976), 168.
4. Augustine, *The Confessions*, trans. Maria Boulding, 113.
5. Ibid., 144.
6. Ibid., 145.
7. Thompson, "Hound of Heaven," 88.

N 2.7 The Straits of the Will

1. Although John titles this chapter "the straits of the will," Kieran Kavanaugh points out that "the afflictions arise from the memory and overflow into the will." *The Collected Works of St. John of the Cross*, trans. Kieran Kavanaugh and Otilio Rodriguez (Washington, D.C.: ICS Publications, 1991), 406.
2. Dante, *Purgatorio*, trans. Robert Hollander and Jean Hollander (New York: Doubleday, 2003), 243.
3. Johnston, *Cloud of Unknowing*, 99.
4. Leo Tolstoy, *Anna Karenina*, trans. Constance Garnett (Cleveland: Fine Editions Press, 1946), 467.

N 2.8–9 The Paradoxes of Transformation

1. T. S. Eliot, "East Coker," in *Four Quartets* (New York: Harcourt Brace Jovanovich, 1971), 27.
2. William Blake, "The Marriage of Heaven and Hell," in *William Blake: The Complete Poems*, ed. Alicia Ostriker (New York: Penguin, 1988), 188.
3. Maise Ward, *Return to Chesterton* (New York: Sheed and Ward, 1952), 36–37.

4. Charles Dickens, *The Pickwick Papers* (New York: Bantam, 1983), 357. If you are over forty years old and are contemplating playing leapfrog, I would advise that you first consult your physician.

5. Quoted from Kathleen Norris, *Amazing Grace: A Vocabulary of Faith* (New York: Riverhead Books, 1998), 32.

6. J. R. R. Tolkien, *The Fellowship of the Ring*, in *The Lord of the Rings* (New York: Ballantine, 1973), 347.

7. Ibid., 173–74.

8. In one of his letters, Tolkien writes the following about Tom Bombadil: "If 'in time' Tom was primeval he was Eldest in Time. . . . He is *master* in a peculiar way: he has no fear, and no desire of possession or domination at all. He merely knows and understands about such things as concern him or his natural little realm." *The Letters of J. R. R. Tolkien*, ed. Humphrey Carpenter (Boston: Houghton Mifflin, 1981), 191–92.

9. Thomas Merton, *Conjectures of a Guilty Bystander* (Garden City, N.Y.: Doubleday, 1966), 140–42. Merton recounts the same incident in *The Sign of Jonas*. "We drove into town with Senator Dawson, a neighbor of the monastery, and all the while I wondered how I would react at meeting once again face to face, the wicked world. I met the world and I found it no longer so wicked after all. Perhaps the things I had resented about the world when I left it were defects of my own that I had projected upon it. Now, on the contrary, I found that everything stirred me with a deep and mute sense of compassion. Perhaps some of the people we saw going about the streets were hard and tough . . . but I did not stop to observe it because I seemed to have lost an eye for the merely exterior detail and to have discovered, instead, a deep sense of respect and love and pity for the souls that such details never fully reveal. I went through the city, realizing for the first time in my life how good are all the people in the world and how much value they have in sight of God." Thomas Merton, *The Sign of Jonas* (New York: Harcourt Brace, 1953), 91–92.

10. William Wordsworth, "Lines Written a Few Miles above Tintern Abbey," in *William Wordsworth*, ed. Stephen Gill (Oxford: Oxford University Press, 1984), 132.

11. Samuel Johnson, "The Vanity of Human Wishes," in *The Poetical Works of Samuel Johnson*, ed. Thomas Park (London: Stanhope, 1811), 22.

12. G. K. Chesterton, *Orthodoxy* (Garden City, N.Y.: Image Books, 1936), 121.

N 2.10 The Burning Log

1. Augustine, *The Confessions,* trans. Maria Boulding, 101–2.
2. Ibid., 156.
3. Dante, *Paradiso,* 2.34–36, trans. Robert Hollander and Jean Hollander (New York: Doubleday, 2007), 37.
4. See Pseudo-Dionysius, the Aeropagite, *Pseudo-Dionysius: The Complete Works,* trans. Colm Luibheid (New York: Paulist Press, 1987), 72.
5. Charles Williams, *The Figure of Beatrice* (New York: Noonday Press, 1961), 160.
6. Ida Görres, *The Hidden Face: A Study of St. Thérèse of Lisieux,* trans. Richard and Clara Winston (New York: Pantheon, 1959), 107.

N 2.11 Fired with Love's Urgent Longings

1. Augustine, *Homilies on the First Epistle of John,* trans. Boniface Ramsey (Hyde Park, N.Y.: New City Press, 2008), 69.
2. Alfred Lord Tennyson, "Mariana," in *Poems of Tennyson,* ed. Jerome H. Buckley (Boston: Houghton Mifflin, 1958), 18.

N 2.12–14 The Imparting of Wisdom and Love

1. "Instinctive affinity" is Thomas R. Heath's translation of the Latin word *connaturalitatem,* which is often translated as connaturality. Heath's translation is found in the Blackfriars edition of the *Summa Theologiae,* vol. 35 (New York: McGraw-Hill, 1972), 165.
2. Josef Pieper, *For the Love of Wisdom: Essays on the Nature of Philosophy,* trans. Roger Wasserman, ed. Berthold Wald (San Francisco: Ignatius Press, 2006), 80.
3. John follows the teaching of Pseudo-Dionysius. "[Angels] receive undiluted the original enlightenment [from God] . . . and pass on to us these revelations, [which have been] fashioned to suit the beholders." Pseudo-Dionysius, the Aeropagite, *Pseudo-Dionysius: The Complete Works,* trans. Colm Luibheid (New York: Paulist Press, 1987), 157.
4. Dante, *Paradiso,* 21.4–5, in *The Divine Comedy,* trans. John Ciardi (New York: Norton, 1970), 521.

5. Ibid., 23.46–48, 536.

6. Nathaniel Hawthorne, *The English Notebooks: 1853–1856*, ed. Thomas Woodson and Bill Ellis (Columbus: Ohio State University Press, 1997), 412–13. Hawthorne's daughter Rose (Mother Mary Alphonsa, Servant of God) "wrote that the account of this incident in the Liverpool workhouse seemed to her to contain the greatest words her father ever wrote." Flannery O'Connor, *Mystery and Manners: Occasional Prose* (New York: Farrar, Straus & Giroux, 1969), 219.

7. Nathaniel Hawthorne, *Our Old Home: A Series of English Sketches* ed. Fredson Bowers (Columbus: Ohio State University Press, 1970), 300–301.

8. Francis de Sales, *Selected Letters*, trans. Elizabeth Stopp (Stella Niagara, N.Y.: DeSales Resource Center, 2011), 68.

N 2.16 Walking Securely

1. C. S. Lewis, *The Screwtape Letters* (New York: Macmillan, 1982), 39.

2. "Telescopic philanthropy" is the title of chapter 4 of *Bleak House*. The chapter is Dickens's criticism of Christian "do-gooders" who are concerned about saving the pagans across the sea, while neglecting the poor children of the London streets. The phrase "telescopic philanthropy" became such a part of the vocabulary of Victorian England that in 1865 (twelve years after the publication of *Bleak House*), *Punch* magazine published a cartoon showing Britannia looking through a telescope at faraway Africa, while a poor begrimed child of the London streets is pulling at her dress. The child says, imploring Britannia, "Please 'm, ain't we black enough to be cared for?"

3. Charles Dickens, *Bleak House* (New York: Penguin, 1971), 86.

4. Ray Bradbury, *The Martian Chronicles* (New York: Bantam, 1977), 78.

5. This homily was given on October 6, 2011, on the feast of St. Bruno, in the Carthusian monastery in the Calabria region of Italy.

N 2.17 Secret Wisdom

1. C. S. Lewis, *Surprised by Joy: The Shape of My Early Years* (New York: Harcourt Brace, 1955), 237.

2. Dante, *Paradiso*, 33.58–64, in *The Divine Comedy*, trans. John Ciardi (New York: Norton, 1970), 599.

3. Benedicta Ward, *The Sayings of the Desert Fathers*, 234.

N 2.18 The Secret Ladder

1. Marcus Aurelius, *Meditations*, trans. Maxwell Staniforth (Baltimore: Penguin, 1964), 115.

2. This perspective corresponds to St. Ignatius of Loyola's advice that we should gather strength during times of consolation to protect ourselves against temptation during periods of desolation. "Let him who is in consolation think how he will bear himself in the desolation which will follow, gathering energy anew for that time" (Rule I: 10). St. Ignatius gives no hint as to what we should "think" about during times of consolation. However, Jules J. Toner, S.J., offers the following suggestions. "We can, first of all, pray to be given courage, strength, and energy when we will need it. We can meditate on some of the truths of faith which will be a source of strength at that time, such as God's fidelity in love or his power. The present spiritual consolation can be a help to this if we do not merely seek to enjoy the sweetness of the gift but also attend to the love and presence of the Giver." Jules J. Toner, *A Commentary on Saint Ignatius' Rules for the Discernment of Spirits* (St. Louis, Mo.: Institute of Jesuit Sources, 1982), 195.

N 2.19–20 The Ladder of Love

1. Augustine, "Ten Homilies on the First Epistle of John," trans. H. Browne, in *The Nicene and Post-Nicene Fathers*, vol. 7 (Grand Rapids, Mich.: Eerdmans, 1956), 485.

2. de Sales, *Introduction to the Devout Life*, 29.

3. For a good treatment of the relationship between *acedia* and magnanimity, see the following: Josef Pieper, *On Hope*, trans. Mary Frances McCarthy (San Francisco: Ignatius Press, 1986), 47–61.

4. Gershen Kaufman, *Shame: The Power of Caring* (Rochester, Vt.: Schenkman, 1985), 8.

5. For a good treatment of the relationship between humility and magnanimity, see Pieper, *On Hope*, 25–31.

N 2.21 Departing in Disguise

1. For a good treatment of the three-layered vesture worn by medieval knights, see Charles Foulkes, *The Armourer and His Craft from the XIth to the XVIth Century* (London: Methuen, 1912), 104–8.

2. For an excellent introduction to the work of René Girard, see Michael Kirwan, *Discovering Girard* (Cambridge, Mass.: Crowley, 2005).

3. Samuel Johnson, *Selected Essays*, ed. David Womersley (New York: Penguin, 2003), 387.

4. René Girard, *Deceit, Desire, and the Novel: Self and Other in Literary Structure*, trans. Yvonne Freccero (Baltimore: Johns Hopkins University Press, 1976), 21.

5. Sinclair Lewis, *Babbitt* (New York: Harcourt Brace, 1950), 113.

6. Lewis, *Screwtape Letters*, 132.

7. Ibid., 59–60.

8. Alfred Adler, *Social Interest: A Challenge to Mankind*, trans. John Linton and Richard Vaughan (New York: Capricorn, 1964), 209.

9. "Scarlet fever" is a term applied humorously (and in a somewhat disparaging fashion) to a priest who has an excessive ambition to become a bishop. The "scarlet" is a reference to the red clothing worn by bishops.

10. Ross Collings, *John of the Cross* (Collegeville, Minn.: Liturgical Press, 1990), 129–30.

11. Augustine, *Teaching Christianity*, trans. Edmund Hill (Hyde Park, N.Y.: New City Press, 1996), 176.

N 2.22–24 My House Being Now All Stilled

1. Bram Stoker, *Dracula* (New York: Bantam, 1981), 16.

2. Ibid., 253.

3. Lewis, *Screwtape Letters*, 147–48.

4. John Milton, *Paradise Lost*, ed. David Scott Kastan (Indianapolis: Hackett, 2005), book 4.11. *Paradise Lost* is one of the most psychologically and spiritually profound treatments of satanic "astuteness" that has ever been written.

5. Alfred Lord Tennyson, "Flower in the Crannied Wall," in *Poems of Tennyson*, ed. Jerome H. Buckley (Boston: Houghton Mifflin, 1958), 351.

6. Augustine, "The Enchiridion on Faith, Hope, and Charity," in *On Christian Belief*, trans. Bruce Harbert (Hyde Park, N.Y.: New City Press, 2005), 278.

7. Quoted in M. M. Philipon, *The Spiritual Doctrine of Elizabeth of the Trinity*, trans. a Benedictine of Stanbrook Abbey (Washington, D.C.: Teresian Charism Press, 1985), 44.

N 2.25 Conclusion

1. Thomas Gray, "Elegy Written in a Country Churchyard," in *Elegy Written in a Country Churchyard and Other Writings* (London: Orion, 1996), 9.

Index

Note: Page numbers followed by n and a number indicate endnotes

see also knowledge
sensual/sensory experiences
of *acedia*, 66–67
desire to feel peaceful, 96
of excessive penance, 53–55
lack of, 88–90
of prayer, 30–33
sought by gluttons, 49–50
see also emotions
sex. *see* lust
Shakespeare, William, 58–59, 209
shame, 5, 209–210
"The Shoddy Lands" (Lewis),
135–137
silence and solitude, 98–99, 192–
195, 198–199, 230, 233–234
sin
concealment of, 12–13
falling in, 106
inclination toward, 6–7
see also *acedia*; avarice; envy;
gluttony; lust; pride
sloth. see *acedia*
solitude and silence, 98–99, 192–
195, 198–199, 230, 233–234
The Spiritual Canticle (John of the
Cross), xvi, 99–100, 114
spiritual collectors, 25–27
spiritual dilettantes, 22–24
spiritual exercises
complacency in, 9–10
failing to perform, 108
pleasure of, 4–5, 53–55
spiritual reality, xiv, xxi–xxii
spiritual senses, 159–161
"Stanzas of the Soul that Rejoices
in Knowing God through
Faith" (John of the Cross), xvi

Stevens, Wallace, 72
Stevenson, Robert Louis, 13
Storr, Anthony, xix
*The Strange Case of Dr. Jekyll and
Mr. Hyde* (Stevenson), 13
suffering, 152–154, 188–191,
201–202, 231
Syncletica, Amma, 198–199

Tavard, George, xvi–xvii
telescopic philanthropy, 190,
244n2
temptations. *see* trials and
temptations
Tennyson, Alfred, 173–174, 230
Teresa of Ávila, St.
on *Confessions*, 4
on consolation, 8, 9
on contemplation, 225–226,
234
on fasting, 54–55
on love of God, 169
on prayer, 32–33
reform of, xv
relationship with Father Pedro,
37–38
on self-knowledge, 104
theological virtues. *see* virtues
Thérèse of Lisieux, St.
on dark night, 152, 153
on God's guidance, 175
on grace, 74–75
on perfection, 75, 111
on practicing virtue, 42
on sin, 106
on transformation, 170–171
Thomas Aquinas, St.

About Us

ICS Publications, based in Washington, D.C., is the publishing house of the Institute of Carmelite Studies (ICS) and a ministry of the Discalced Carmelite Friars of the Washington Province (U.S.A.). The Institute of Carmelite Studies promotes research and publication in the field of Carmelite spirituality, especially about Carmelite saints and related topics. Its members are friars of the Washington Province.

The Discalced Carmelites are a worldwide Roman Catholic religious order comprised of friars, nuns, and laity—men and women who are heirs to the teaching and way of life of Teresa of Avila and John of the Cross, dedicated to contemplation and to ministry in the church and the world.

Information about their way of life is available through local diocesan vocation offices, or from the Discalced Carmelite Friars vocation directors at the following addresses:

Washington Province:
1525 Carmel Road, Hubertus, WI 53033

California-Arizona Province:
P.O. Box 3420, San Jose, CA 95156

Oklahoma Province:
5151 Marylake Drive, Little Rock, AR 72206

Visit our websites at:

www.icspublications.org and *http://ocdfriarsvocation.org*